TREVOR'S SONG

The MIRACULOUS TRUE STORY
of GOD'S HEALING POWER
after a TRAGIC FARM ACCIDENT

T. A. BEAM

MILESTONES
INTERNATIONAL PUBLISHERS

TREVOR'S SONG: The Miraculous True Story of God's Healing Power after a Tragic Farm Accident

ISBN: 978-0-924748-99-8
UPC: 88571300069-7

Milestones International Publishers
PO Box 104
Newburg, PA 17240
PH: 303.503.7257
FAX: 717.477.2261

www.milestonesintl.com

Cover design: Knail

Some names, places and events have been changed to protect the innocent.

1 2 3 4 5 6 7 8 / 13 12 11 10 09

DEDICATION

This book is dedicated to God. We often refer to Him as our "Daddy in Heaven" who surrounds us with His protection, encompasses us with His healing, and is with us in every situation. Our **prayer** is that this book will bring encouragement, strength and healing to every reader, as well as ignite a new passion in your Christian walk. Our **promise** is to share His story, His love, and His healing power with the world.

ACKNOWLEDGMENTS

Words cannot express our gratitude for the swift and professional response of all emergency personnel, from the EMTs first on the scene, to Life Lion, to the doctors and nurses who cared so well for Trevor during his stay at the hospital. Your professionalism, compassion and sincere concern is appreciated beyond words.

A very special thanks to Dr. Boustred. You touched our lives. Having a Doctor as you, that has such a great love for God our father and our Lord and Savior Jesus Christ, added with your words "...I'm just his hands, It is God that does the healing..." gave us even more comfort and peace and strengthened our faith in a time of tragedy. The Bible says *"Again I say unto you, That if two of you shall agree on earth as touching any thing that they shall ask, it shall be done for them of my Father which is in heaven. For where two or three are gathered together in my name, there am I in the midst of them."* (Matthew 18:19-20, KJV) We as a family ask God to Bless you and your family in a special way. Thank you for your support, both as a doctor and a Christian brother.

As for me and my house, we will serve the Lord. A very special thank you to my parents for their prayers and comfort and always being there to help with the younger children. Thank you to TJ and Trent for continuing on with the chores and being strong. Thank you Tiffany, Tyler, Travis and Tiara for just being there for daddy to love and encouraging Trevor. And a very special thank you to the rest of my family and friends for your prayers and staying strong, positive and faithful. Thank you for your sacrifices. Most of all, thank you for believing in a God of miracles. What could have been a season of tragic mourning and loss is now and forevermore a time of joy and celebration.

And to Trevor; thank you for holding on and staying strong. Your unwavering belief in me, your daddy, has strengthened my trust in my Daddy in Heaven.

A very special thank you to Larry Walker for your writing and editorial support.

Thanks also to James Rill, of Milestones International Publishers, for inspiring us to write the book and for all your help, support and encouragement through the process. We value you as a special friend.

And thanks most of all to my Heavenly Father and my Lord and Savior Jesus Christ for saving my son's life and giving him complete healing.

As a matter of fact, the photograph of the boy running on the front cover is actually of Trevor just months after the accident.

THANK YOU JESUS!!!

ENDORSEMENT

Trevor's story contains all the ingredients of a true miracle! Jesus did so many of His miracles when He was moved with compassion. When a family is faced with the possibility of such incredible loss, they can be moved by fear or love and compassion. Trevor's family was moved by the latter. Their love for Trevor and their trust for God facilitated the emergence of compassion over fear.

Like most real miracles, Trevor's miracle didn't happen in a church. It wasn't one sensational prayer or a single sweeping event. It was a journey. Real life is always a journey. His journey involved faith, doctors, compassion and challenge. And in the struggles of real life, a real family walks through a miracle.

In Trevor's story you'll see why it is so incredibly important for Jesus to be the root of our life. In real life crisis there is never time to go back and fill your lamp with oil. In real life what you really have is expressed effortlessly and naturally. You'll be inspired! You'll cry! You'll be riveted to these pages. But in the end, you'll sink your roots deeper into the safety of a loving God!

Dr. James B. Richards, PhD, ThD
Best-Selling Author of *Breaking the Cycle, Anatomy of a Miracle*

FOREWORD

"I first met Trevor the 10th of January 2008. As the attending plastic surgeon on call I was called to the operating room to help evaluate and recommend a course of action for a young boy with severe injuries to his lower limbs. The pediatric surgeons had taken him urgently to the operating room to evaluate his injuries and commence treatment under anesthesia. Trevor had suffered extensive degloving injuries to both of his legs, skin was missing or badly damaged over large areas, 2 of the 3 blood vessels in the one leg were torn out, and the third one badly damaged, with blood supply to the foot in jeopardy and there was significant injury to muscles. Having examined Trevor, I called in the vascular surgeon for their additional expertise. With a severe injury like this the difficult decision is whether to attempt to reconstruct or to amputate. Attempting to reconstruct a badly damaged limb can lead to severe complications (e.g. infection) and there is no guarantee of success.

The pediatric surgeon and I donned gloves and quickly located Troy Beam, Trevor's dad, in the family waiting area, whom we were meeting for the first time. We wanted to discuss Trevor's injuries and options for treatment, and both of us felt that amputation was a course of action that might be necessary. These meetings with the family are always difficult. As a surgeon, I need to explain the situation in layman's terms, give options for treatment, maintain objectivity, forge a relationship with the family and support and encourage them in their time of crisis. The family has to make difficult and objective decisions in their highly traumatized and emotional state. We explained the extent and nature of the injuries to Troy. He was understandably very upset at the possibility of amputation. My heart went out to this man who had experienced every father's dread—he had witnessed his son's terrible injury, and had personally carried his badly injured son away from the scene of the accident. Troy declared his faith in God, and in God's ability to perform miracles and transform disasters, and he asked us not to amputate, but to do everything possible to try and save Trevor's leg.

As a follower of Jesus Christ, I was delighted to learn of the Beam families' love for God and trust in Christ. This enabled me as Trevor's caregiver to take the doctor-patient relationship to a deeper level. I offered to pray with Troy for wisdom and for the Almighty's guidance, and for His hand to be present in the surgeries and to give us, the surgeons, skill. We three prayed together in that busy patient waiting area, the pediatric surgeon, Troy and I, and God forged a deep relationship between us at that moment.

Trevor required several operations, firstly revascularization of his leg—the vascular surgeon performed an arterial bypass, the wounds were thoroughly debrided and stabilized. He later underwent extensive skin grafting following further debridements. Trevor recovered wonderfully—he developed none of the myriad of possible complications, such as infection, blockage of the arterial reconstruction, loss of skin grafts, contractures of the joints and so on. His pain control was easy, his attitude was remarkable. Staff came to comfort Trevor and his family, but instead left the bedside finding themselves encouraged and uplifted by the Beam family. Their faith in Gods' ability to heal Trevor of these terrible injuries, and help him walk again was remarkable. Their positive, yet down-to-earth approach to this crisis in their lives was inspiring to all of us who took care of Trevor, and even the most cynical staff members found themselves strangely warmed by their encounters with this family.

Did God perform a miracle? Trevor made a remarkable recovery, no complications, and a functional result that I did not anticipate or believe was possible given the extent of his injuries. It is true that with the wonders of modern medicine and skilled treatment we are able to achieve results that hitherto were not possible. Children have the most amazing ability to heal, and accomplish greater degrees of recovery than adults with an equivalent injury. Perhaps these factors account for Trevor's recovery. However, he has achieved a degree of rehabilitation we did not think possible, and having witnessed the injury, the faith of this young boy and his family, the smooth course post-operatively and his amazing functional recovery, I have to believe that God has played a significant role in this result. Having been trained in the scientific method and rigorous examination of facts and data, I cannot say that there is unequivocal evidence of divine intervention in the form of a physical miracle of healing. However Trevor's remarkable recovery and the attitude and grace displayed by his family, are testament to God's presence in their lives. He is the One who is able to take us beyond ourselves, who enables us to accomplish far more than we can hope for, to bear more than we believe possible. His presence permeates our lives and beings. Our bodies are wonderfully designed and made and I know that He played the greatest role in orchestrating all factors to work for best in Trevor's healing and recovery."

Dr. Boustred

MD, FACS, FCS(SA), FRCS(Ed), FCS(Plast)

Dr. Boustred is a fellow of the American College of Surgeons and an Associate Member of the American Society of Plastic Surgeons. Dr Boustred is also a member of the following Societies for Plastic Surgeons in the USA: Jurkiewicz Society (Emory University), American Cleft Palate—Craniofacial Association, American Society of Maxillo-Facial Surgeons, Ivy Society Plastic Surgeons (Pennsylvania), Northeastern Society of Plastic Surgeons and the Christian Medical and Dental Society. He is also a member of the International Society of Aesthetic Plastic Surgeons.

Dr. Boustred was born and raised in South Africa. He received his medical degree at the University Witwatersrand (a 6 year course) followed by internship at the Johannesburg academic hospital. His surgical residency of 5 years was at the University of Cape Town/Groote Schuur Hospital. A Neurosurgery fellowship completed this phase of his training and prepared him for medical mission work in Lesotho. He returned to a faculty position at the University of Cape Town academic hospital as an attending surgeon. After several years in this position, he decided to train in Plastic Surgery, completing another 3 years of residency at the same university hospital, including a full year in Pediatric Plastic Surgery. He completed additional (optional) training in Plastic Surgery at the prestigious unit at Emory University Hospital under the mentorship of Professors John Bostwick and Foad Nahai.

Dr. Boustred's special interests include pediatric and craniofacial surgery, cleft lip and palate, conditions affecting the face, both reconstructive and cosmetic, oculoplastic surgery and breast surgery. He does, however, enjoy the wide range of procedures offered by plastic surgery and practices the broad scope of the specialty.

Dr. Boustred has spent 3 years doing medical mission work in Namibia, Zululand and Lesotho. On completing his Plastic Surgery training he returned to South Africa to part-time academic practice and private practice. With deteriorating conditions in South Africa he accepted a position in New Zealand at the academic hospital of the University of Otago in Christchurch, spending a year and a half in that beautiful country. He was then recruited back to the USA, to train Plastic Surgery residents at Penn State University/Hershey Medical Centre, where he has been for 7 years up till June 2008, as an Associate Professor in Plastic Surgery and Ophthalmology, and Co-Director of the Craniofacial Unit. He is now in private practice in Fort Collins, Colorado.

TABLE OF CONTENTS

PREFACE

The story I am about to tell you is not about me. It's not about my wife or my children. And despite its title, it's not about our son Trevor. This story is about a Savior, the Lord Jesus Christ. He is real, He is my God, and He is alive. In this life there is a separation so that we cannot see His face; in fact, we probably could not handle seeing His face. But He is real. I know He is real; it is my prayer that by the time you finish reading this book, you, too, will know that He is real.

How do I know Christ is real? Because I have a little boy who is alive today but shouldn't be; a little boy who is running again when nobody thought he would walk; a little boy whom I thought I had found dead.

Jesus said, *"For many are called, but few are chosen"* (Matthew 22:14). In another place, He issued this sober warning:

Not every one that saith unto me, Lord, Lord, shall enter into the kingdom of heaven; but he that doeth the will of my Father which is in heaven.

Many will say to me in that day, Lord, Lord, have we not prophesied in thy name? and in thy name have cast out devils? and in thy name done many wonderful works?

3

*And then will I profess unto them, I never knew you: depart from
me, ye that work iniquity.*

— Matthew 7:21-23

Whenever I read that Scripture, I have to search my heart. Those
words make me want to draw closer to Him. I don't want to do "many
wonders"; I don't want to put on the right costume; I don't want to say
all the right words; I don't want to take all the right steps; I don't want
to look the right way—only to end up in eternity and hear the words,
"I never knew you; depart from Me." That would be tragic! It would be
for eternity—forever and ever and ever. There's no turning back from
a devil's hell when we leave this world without Christ.

Trevor's accident has made me realize this more than ever before.
I hope and pray that your heart will remain open as I share with you
a story that came from God. It's a story of His power, His goodness,
and His love.

Troy leaned against a fence post, pulled off his leather work gloves, and wiped the perspiration from his eyes as he grinned at his son. Trevor, for his part, brushed the grass off of his knees and poked a finger in the new hole that had mysteriously appeared in his jeans.

"I'll vouch for you with Mommy, Trevor. You earned that hole in your jeans the honest way—by helping Daddy all day long with this fence line. Thanks for being there for me, son."

Trevor grinned and said, "You were there for me when I really needed you the most, Dad."

That was all it took to melt Troy's heart. He instinctively drew Trevor close in a warm hug as memories of his son's brush with death and of God's faithfulness over the previous year flooded his mind.

"You know, we have a lot to be thankful for, son. God was with us, no matter how dark things looked at the time. It was our Daddy in Heaven who surrounded us with His grace and mercy. And it was our Daddy in Heaven who healed you. When we called he was always there for us."

Trevor tightened his grip and looked into his daddy's face.

"You know what, Dad? I think He is a lot like you," he said shyly as he glanced at the sun's rays piercing the thick clouds overhead.

Trevor's mind went back to the day he came home and said "That's why I told that nurse who thought you wouldn't make it because of the storm, 'You don't know my dad,' I knew you would come for me ... "

CHAPTER ONE

"OH, LORD, PLEASE SAVE HIS LIFE!"

The dispatcher stared at her empty coffee cup, wondering if she should pour another. The hot brew was a welcome warmth that crisp Thursday morning at Life Lion Critical Care in central Pennsylvania.

Maybe we'll get a quiet morning, she thought, *one that will give me time to take down these Christmas cards still cluttering my desk ten days into January.*

She had barely reached for the first card when the 9-1-1 line crackled over her headset and the digital dispatch board lit up. The words she heard next sent a chill down her spine.

"This is Pennsylvania 9-1-1 dispatch calling Life Lion Critical Care. PSP [Pennsylvania State Police] requests emergency heli evac, Shippensburg borough. Farm accident involving juvenile male, age 8. Potential life-threatening injuries to trunk, lower

extremities. Meet EMT at farm—precise location to follow. Penn State Hershey [Medical Center] alerted to incoming pediatric trauma victim and standing by."

Despite taking hundreds of emergency crisis calls a month, she felt a cold uneasiness creep over her. A farm accident. An eight-year-old boy. Life-threatening injuries. This was a bad one.

Pennsylvania is a historic and heavily populated state with a number of very large cities renowned around the world. It also supports a prolific farming culture with hundreds of thousands of dairy, beef, pork, and feed grain farms. They range from large corporate operations to countless family-owned farms made famous by the state's concentration of Mennonite and Amish farming communities.

Virtually all of these farms must use heavy equipment to conduct their operations—whether they are powered by state-of-the-art diesel-powered tractors or circa 17th-century teams of draft horses. Where there is farm machinery, there is an ever-present danger of catastrophic accidents. And the worst of the worst involve farm children.

Within less than a minute, the dispatcher had alerted the three-member flight crew for Life Lion 2, the critical care helicopter based in Carlisle, Pennsylvania, which was closer to the accident site.

The dispatcher couldn't see the faces of the concerned flight crew members scurrying to lift off 30 miles away, but she didn't have to. She knew each member of that flight team was experiencing feelings of dread as they prepared for takeoff. Farm accidents of any nature were almost always horrific and, much too often, fatal.

The pilot hurried to file a flight plan as the flight nurse and flight paramedic hastily gathered specialized gear for the trauma case described in the call. They ran to the helipad.

Within minutes, the crew completed their preflight checklist and the dark blue body of Life Lion 2 lifted from the helipad and disappeared from sight on a southwest heading over Pennsylvania's crowded Interstate 81 corridor.

Thursday morning dawned cold and overcast with thick, gray clouds over the Beam farm in south central Pennsylvania. Yet, the key wasn't the weather; it was the dawn. Every farm family knows that whether a new day dawns cold or hot, brings endless sheets of rain, or shines down parching drought conditions, there are animals to be fed and always work that must be done.

Troy Beam already had planned his day by the time the sun rose that morning at 7:30, but he made sure his three oldest boys were up and moving toward the barn by 8:00 a.m.

T.J., Trent, and Trevor, his oldest sons, grabbed their coats and worn work boots before they headed for the barn under Dad's watchful eye. Today they had planned to chop some of the winter oats that were still on their stalks. Troy wanted the beef cows fed before too much of the day had slipped away, and he was watching the driveway for a client scheduled to come early that morning to discuss a construction project.

Meanwhile, Debbie Beam began another day as the matriarch of the growing Beam household. The baby in her womb was in its first trimester, but she really couldn't slow down to accommodate the changes in her body. She was too busy keeping up with her seven children who were growing up right before her eyes.

On this particular morning, Debbie realized she still hadn't adjusted to seeing her third son, Trevor, dash out of the kitchen to do "men's chores" with his older brothers. It seemed just yesterday that Trevor was the proud leader of the younger pack, his smaller siblings following him through the breakfast routine each morning. He used to be a key motivator for the young ones as they prepared for the homeschooling schedule that dominated their focus each week. Now he was busy doing "men's work" with the men of the house. *Where has the time gone?* she mused.

The kitchen was filled with laughter as the younger children played together. Debbie smiled at the energy of her younger division of the "T" team: Tiffany, Tyler, Travis, and Tiara.

Even before she married Troy Beam, she knew from her growing relationship with him that the letter "T" would probably play an important role in her life. She had no idea that it would be the first letter in the names of all of her children. (She and Troy would have to come up with the eighth "T" name in just a few months.)

With a satisfaction that seemed to go all the way down to her toes, she smiled and silently thought, *Healthy children are a blessing.*

Tiffany, Trevor's twin and the oldest girl, was sitting on the floor feeding a graham cracker to 13-month-old chubby-cheeked Tiara. The odor of slightly scorched toast revealed that Tyler, a fun-loving four-year-old, had finally grown tall enough to help with the task. At the moment, though, Tyler had pinned two-year-old Travis to the floor in a friendly wrestling match. The sizzling noise of frying bacon added to the general hubbub of activity.

The smell of fried bacon had permeated the entire house by the time Troy's client arrived to discuss some building and remodeling business. Since her questions required information he kept in his home office, he took her inside, leaving the boys to continue unloading the silage.

It was a routine job—one they had performed many times before. Routine, however, did not necessarily mean safe. Since the Beams were feeding *large* farm animals, they handled a high volume of feed every day. And that meant machinery.

Just a week earlier, Troy had taken the opportunity to once again remind the boys of the dangers inherent in the "routine" farm work when he noticed some potentially unsafe work habits around the equipment they were using. The boys were chopping winter oats and unloading them from a self-unloading forage wagon when it jammed.

This tall, four-wheeled wagon was pulled and powered by a tractor and was used to haul, cut, and unload feed for storage or for easy access by livestock.

The wagon was a self-unloading version with a chain-driven bed or conveyor-like floor that moved the silage toward the front of the wagon and the three sets of metal beater bars mounted there. Each beater was fitted with rotating prongs to grab, separate, shred, and evenly distribute the harvested feed during the unloading process. This particular wagon featured a shield on one side to keep the silage from falling onto the ground.

On that day a week prior, silage had piled up between the shield and the conveyor and jammed while Troy was inside the house.

The boys wanted to clear the jam, but before they approached the operating wagon they remembered to shut off the power takeoff (PTO). Troy had warned them *never* to get close to the wagon when the power takeoff drive was running. However, they forgot to shut down the tractor.

The boys climbed into the wagon to clear the silage jam just as Troy returned to the wagon. He immediately noticed that the tractor was running and the boys were nowhere in sight. Instinctively, he knew they had climbed into the wagon and were standing on the moving conveyor *right next to the beaters!* A chill of fear shot through Troy's body.

He dashed to the tractor and shut it down before calling out to his sons. "Boys, you come down here right now!"

T.J., Trent, and Trevor climbed out of the wagon and sheepishly walked over to their father, knowing they deserved what they were about to hear. Troy shook his head and sternly looked into the eyes of each of the boys.

Then he pointed at the self-unloading silage wagon and said, "I don't ever want to see you in the back of that wagon when it is hooked up to the tractor with the engine running! That wagon is dangerous. If you get caught in those beaters, they will kill you. I know you boys are tough, but you're not tougher than those beaters."

T.J., Trent, and Trevor were 12, 10, and 8, respectively. *The trouble with boys that age, Troy thought to himself, is that you're never sure whether they hear you or not.* He thought of his own responses to his concerned father during his younger days and made a decision.

Although his boys were confident in their abilities and were motivated to do their jobs well and do them efficiently, at times they could move instinctively instead of thoughtfully.

Just to be safe, Troy removed the shield from the wagon so it wouldn't jam up again. It was designed to prevent the spilling of animal feed, but unfortunately, sometimes it seemed to contribute to the kind of equipment jam that triggered "instinctive" and dangerous actions by young workers. Troy cared a whole lot more about his sons' safety than a little lost feed.

He said nothing more to the boys about the episode that morning, hoping that his reprimand would be sufficient.

Now, a week later on another January morning, it felt good to work together again with his sons, even though the "thrill" of unloading the stringy, smelly silage from the forage wagon had come and gone a long time ago. The air was brisk and cold, punctuated by their frosty breath as they worked.

Nevertheless, as Troy walked to the house to talk with the potential client that morning, the jamming incident of the previous week wasn't far from his mind. He led the customer to his home office and had barely begun to discuss the project when T.J. suddenly burst into the room.

"Dad, come quick! *Trevor's stuck in the wagon!*"

Troy's heart sank. He didn't need to hear anything more. He already knew beyond a doubt that Trevor was in serious trouble. He mumbled a quick apology to the woman as he exploded from his chair and rushed toward the door.

In his mind, he was screaming, "Father in heaven! Help Trevor! He's only eight!" Even before Troy cleared the chair, his mind was firing off questions at lightning speed.

What had possessed Trevor to make him climb inside that wagon?

Did he think he could push the oats into the beaters?

Dear God, how did this happen?

Troy rushed so quickly to get outside to Trevor that one sleeve of his long-sleeved shirt caught on a part of the door frame and nearly ripped it off his shoulder. He ignored it and just kept running.

He couldn't see anything from the door of the house—the wagon was on the other side of the barn. As Troy hit the ground and sprinted toward the barn, he felt as if he was moving in slow motion. He glanced over his shoulder to see Debbie running about 50 yards behind him.

She had been standing in the kitchen when she saw T.J. running past the window, a look of horror on his face. A few seconds later, Troy bolted past the same window in the direction of the barn. Instinctively, she knew something was terribly wrong and that it had to do with one of the children. In less time than a blink of an eye, she took off after Troy.

As Troy rounded the corner of the barn, he finally saw the wagon — *and Trevor.*

He was fearing the worst all the way from the house to the wagon. Now that he could see his son, he knew his fear was justified.

Trevor seemed to be lying motionless on top of the stilled beater bars. It was obvious that he had been pulled through the machinery once already, and would have gone through again had his brothers not intervened and turned off the tractor.

Troy stood transfixed for one brief moment. In stunned silence, his eyes seemed to be riveted to the horrifying sight, but he couldn't believe what he was seeing.

The very next moment, he found himself *beside Trevor* inside the silage wagon! (In the days that followed, he couldn't figure out how he moved from a standing position several yards away from the wagon to the place inside the wagon's man-high walls on a conveyor floor about two feet above the ground. It seemed humanly impossible to close that distance and scale the side of that tall forage wagon so quickly.)

"Dad, Dad!" Trent, the 10-year-old, cried out. "Help me get him off!"

14

Trent had stayed at Trevor's side while his oldest brother went for help. Only God knew what went through his tender mind as he stared at his little brother's body, just hoping for a miracle during those long and lonely moments in the wagon.

Troy moved closer to Trevor and instantly realized the situation was far worse than he had first feared. His little boy was lying on top of the metal beater bars with his eyes closed, his head lying sideways, and his mouth hanging open.

He saw no movement and no apparent signs of life. All the clothing from his waist down had been stripped completely away. It was clear from evidence at the scene that the mechanized beaters had squeezed Trevor's abdomen with nearly deadly force.

Then Troy saw Trevor's legs.

"Oh, Lord," he cried out in anguish. "Please, just save his life!"

The flesh on both of Trevor's lower legs had been ripped away, his muscles completely exposed. What little of the flesh that remained was dangling down around his ankle.

Is he dead? Troy wondered frantically. *Oh, no, Lord! Please, no!*

Then, as he carefully lifted Trevor off of the beater bars and cradled him to his chest, Troy thought he heard a small sound come from his seemingly lifeless little boy.

Fearing that Trevor had just taken his final breath, Troy drew his son even closer into his arms and cried out, "Please save his life, Lord!"

By this time Trent had arrived with the uniloader, a small, low-profile farm tractor with a large front bucket. Trent moved the tractor bucket toward the drop-down gate at the rear of the wagon, and Troy struggled to gently clear Trevor's seemingly lifeless body from the beaters and get him to ground level. Just when Troy was about to step out of the wagon and put him into the elevated bucket, all the while crying out to God, he heard a wonderful sound.

A weak voice said, "Daddy, am I going to be all right?" Trevor looked up at his father with a clear gaze.

A wave of relief washed over Troy. Trevor was *alive!* "Trevor," he said, trying to keep his voice calm, "you're going to be fine. Daddy's going to take good care of you."

By this time Debbie had reached the wagon, her eyes wide with fear and her face ashen. "Don't look in here," Troy warned her. "It's bad. Call 9-1-1 and tell them it's bad!"

Without a word, she spun around and ran back toward the house, her bare feet pounding the stones on the farm lane. Her son's very life was at stake.

Troy didn't really want to put Trevor into that dirty tractor bucket because it was used for farmyard duties every day, and Trevor's legs were literally raw and terribly exposed. Yet, he also knew that every lost minute could decrease his son's chances for survival, and it was a long run to the house.

At that moment, he made up his mind. Trevor's legs were a secondary concern; the thing that mattered the most was saving Trevor's life. Shaking his head, he started to put Trevor into the tractor bucket, but as he moved closer to the bucket, the loose part of Trevor's leg fell onto the ground.

To Troy's horror, one of the farm dogs noticed the body part and started sniffing at it. "Get away from there!" Troy warned the animal, still cradling Trevor in his arms. "If you eat that leg, you're dead!"

Desperate to get Trevor inside, Troy decided to ignore the uniloader. He quickly scooped up the leg tissue from the ground and gripped Trevor tightly to him. Then he filled his lungs to capacity and ran for the house with his precious cargo, knowing every step of the way that the clock of life was ticking …

At the house T.J. was already talking to the 9-1-1 operator on the cordless phone. Debbie snatched the phone from him and cried into the receiver, "Please, come as quick as you can! It's really bad! He's going to die if you don't hurry!"

The woman in the office had come outside, and after viewing Troy rushing toward the house with his mangled, bloody son in his arms, even physically brushing past her, she quietly got in her car and left. (Later she told the Beams that she had to pull her car off to the side of the road and call her boss. She felt as if she could faint and didn't know if she could make it to work.)

Trevor hadn't made a sound since Troy had reassured him everything would be all right. Troy's emotions raced as fast as his heart as he cleared the kitchen doorway and laid Trevor on the island.

Troy leaned against the cupboard countertop trying to catch his breath, noticing for the first time that his one remaining sleeve and entire front of his shirt was stained bright red with his son's blood. Then, to his shock, he noticed that Trevor was holding up his head!

"Lie down and relax, Trevor," he encouraged him. "Don't get excited." He felt it was important to calm his son and limit all physical exertion or excitement. He didn't know how much blood Trevor had lost, but judging from the condition of his legs, there was a very real possibility he could bleed to death before any medical help could arrive.

Despite Troy's urging, Trevor insisted, "Put a pillow under my head."

"I will," Troy replied. "Just lie down and don't get excited."

Yet, Trevor was emphatic. "I want a *pillow* under my head!"

It was clear that Trevor would not lay his head down until he had a pillow, so Troy looked over his shoulder and nodded to one of the older boys who had come into the kitchen. "Go get him a pillow."

It took only a few seconds for the pillow to arrive, and Trevor finally laid down his head. Only then did Troy notice the large gash that ran across the top of Trevor's head. *Now I know why Trevor wanted the pillow,* he thought to himself.

Meanwhile, Debbie finally completed her tense conversation with 9-1-1, but not until she felt the people on the other end of the line understood how urgent Trevor's condition was. She wearily replaced the phone in its charger, massaged her stiffening neck for a moment, and walked into the kitchen.

"Help is on the way," she said with relief in her voice. "They'll be here soon ... "

That was when she approached the island and saw Trevor's injuries for the first time. Her eyes widened in horror and one hand flew involuntarily to her mouth.

At first, Troy thought Debbie was going to break down, but she didn't. Debbie was strong like that; it was one of the many things he loved about her. He knew in his gut that she would need every ounce of strength that God had given her to complete the journey they had just begun.

Debbie quickly regained her composure by focusing all of her being on her little boy lying on the kitchen island. She managed a smile and moved closer to gaze at Trevor through tear-glistened eyes.

Gently stroking his head with one hand, she softly said, "It's all right, Trevor. Everything's going to be all right."

CHAPTER TWO

"YOU DON'T BELONG HERE. GET GOING!"

Beautiful, blue-eyed Tiffany, Trevor's twin sister, had been born a mere 20 minutes later than her brother. Despite her second-place arrival, she possessed a strong personality and equally strong maternal instincts.

Tiffany's direct link to Trevor in heart and spirit was evident from the moment they were brought together at birth. This heartbreaking moment was no exception.

When she heard the commotion and realized that Trevor was hurt, a deep fear pressed her to simply disappear and avoid any painful news of his injuries. But another part of her personality—the dominant part of her being—refused to give in and hide.

Then Tiffany saw her daddy running toward the kitchen with Trevor in his arms. She instantly noticed there was a lot of blood. She also realized with a shock that somehow the accident had stripped away all of her brother's clothing from the waist down.

She whirled around and quickly gathered up the younger children to herd them out of the kitchen. "Come with me to the living room, quickly. Trevor's been hurt and we need to pray for him. Everything is going to be all right. Sit down right here and be still; that way Daddy and Mommy can help Trevor."

Even before the kitchen door opened, Tiffany could hear her father's heavy footsteps and his labored breathing. After the door slammed shut, she listened to the odd collection of sounds and understood instinctively that her father was laying Trevor on the kitchen island. When Tiffany overheard her mother's gasp, she knew she just had to sneak a peek at Trevor. Turning to the younger children, she sternly ordered them to stay put.

Tiffany was still holding little Tiara, who was too young to be left by herself on the living room couch. As the eight-year-old moved toward the kitchen, she carefully positioned the toddler so she wouldn't see Trevor on the kitchen island.

Twin sister Tiffany watched her mother gently caress Trevor's face with one hand, speaking so softly that she could barely understand the words. And when Debbie quickly wiped away tears with the other hand so her son wouldn't notice them, Tiffany quietly struggled to control her own flood of tears and growing concern.

As Debbie comforted Trevor, Troy did his best to hide his dismay while examining Trevor's terrible injuries. He'd worked on farms and in the construction business all of his life. Although he had seen and heard of some horrendous injuries in those occupations, he never dreamed that he would witness something so awful happen to his very own, precious son.

Both of the boy's legs from the bend of his knee down to his heels had been stripped of skin. They looked like a picture from an anatomy chart. Bone, tendons, and raw muscle were clearly visible on both legs.

"Straighten out my leg!" Trevor said to his daddy.

"Just a minute, Trevor, okay? Just a minute. Daddy will help you." Troy hastily examined the shredded legs, trying to determine if he should tie a tourniquet above Trevor's knees. But amazingly enough, there didn't seem to be any major blood loss. He was slightly puzzled but came around to Trevor's crooked left leg. Debbie was standing at Trevor's head, intently watching the boy trying to move his leg to a more comfortable position.

"Oh, Troy, look! I think it's broken," she whispered ever so softly, not wanting her son to hear. Troy watched as Trevor tried in vain to move the leg again. Only the upper part of his femur would move, while the rest of the leg dangled uselessly.

He felt a wave of emotional pain surge through his chest that was almost physical in its severity. *Why couldn't it have been me?* he cried silently to the Lord.

Tiffany's intense focus on her parents and injured twin was broken when she felt a tug on her dress. She looked around to find two sets of little eyes fixed on her. Tyler, who was 4 going on 14, and two-year-old Travis just had to know what was going on. Their little voices whispered simultaneously, "What happened? Is Trevor going to be all right? We want to see him!"

"Shhh! Don't bother Daddy and Mommy right now!" Tiffany told the kids in an urgent whisper. "They're trying to help Trevor, and we have to help, too, by being quiet for awhile."

Troy and Debbie slowly and gingerly straightened Trevor's crooked left leg, watching for any sign that they had moved too fast or even a fraction of an inch in the wrong direction. It was only after they felt reassured Trevor was more comfortable that they started to examine both legs again.

Then the emergency response team raced up the drive, lights flashing, only ten minutes after the family's urgent 9-1-1 call. It is difficult to describe just how significant and even miraculous it is to have such a rapid response in a far-flung farming community boasting few direct roads and hundreds of meandering and potentially confusing back roads.

The men entered the kitchen in a rush, throwing their satchels on the floor and pulling on plastic gloves. They rapidly fired questions at Troy and Debbie in an attempt to understand exactly what had happened to the little boy who lay silently watching them.

"What kind of machinery did he get caught in?"

"It was a silage unloading wagon. A forage wagon."

"What part of it did he get caught in?"

"The front of it has three beater bars, one on top of the other, that have prongs about the size of your thumb. When I found him, he was lying on the top beater bar. He must've went through it once and was getting ready to go around again."

The EMT shuddered as he fumbled in his satchel for scissors.

"What kept him from going around again?" he asked, expertly cutting through the sleeve of Trevor's heavy coat.

Troy's blue eyes met those of his tall 12-year-old son, T.J., who stood by a wide-eyed Trent.

"Tell them what happened, boys."

T.J. looked at Trent for a long moment. Then he took a deep breath.

"Well, we saw his shoes come out of the chute and about that same time, I heard him screaming." His voice held a slight tremor. "I ran to the tractor and shut it down."

"I tried to pull his coat away from his neck," Trent almost whispered, "because it looked like it was choking him."

"You're one lucky boy, Trevor," the EMT told him cheerfully. "I believe those brothers of yours saved your life today."

As the EMTs examined Trevor, they were just as surprised as Troy had been to find that they didn't need a tourniquet to staunch the bleeding despite the significant injury to his lower extremities. (This truly was remarkable because, as the family learned later, two of the three main blood vessels providing oxygenated blood to Trevor's foot had been ripped completely out in the accident, and the only remaining vessel was clearly damaged.)

After the initial examination, the medics talked gently to Trevor to calm him as they put a collar brace around his neck. At this point, they knew there was no way of knowing the full extent of his injuries, especially any hidden internal or spinal injuries. He had a head injury, but they didn't know if his neck had been injured as well in such a violent accident. They were taking no chances.

One thing was clear to each member of the EMT crew: Trevor was in critical condition. The graphic evidence on display on that kitchen island was all they needed to verify their conclusion. They carefully passed along the results of their on-site examination via radio to unseen trauma specialists waiting for Trevor's arrival.

Troy and Debbie wouldn't learn until later that in the opinion of most of the medical professionals who examined Trevor that day, there was no way to save his right leg because it was so severely mangled by the harvester beaters and prongs. Bones and tendons in both of Trevor's legs were exposed, but most of the muscle and flesh on his right leg was shredded, down at his ankle, or gone!

"Where are you going to take Trevor?" Troy asked, trying to figure out which regional hospital was closest and yet best equipped to save Trevor's life and the use of his limbs.

"Don't worry," one of the EMTs replied. "Life Lion is on the way. We called them *as soon as we heard it was a farm accident.*"

A farm accident…yes, this would definitely qualify as one of those especially horrendous emergencies requiring the best medical care available in the shortest period of time, thought Troy.

Life Lion was a critical care service funded through the medical center called Penn State Hershey. The service sends emergency teams by helicopter throughout south central Pennsylvania to transport critically ill or accident victims in severe, life-threatening trauma to area hospitals and medical centers.

The EMT literally saw some of the raw tension drain from the faces of the older members of the Beam family when they heard that the Life Lion helicopter was on its way. It seemed to inject some much needed hope into the seemingly hopeless situation.

Almost immediately, Troy went to the kitchen door and called out in a loud voice for T.J. and Trent, who had walked outside. He had been piloting a private plane for many years and had constructed an airstrip right there on the property. As soon as the boys arrived, he told them, "Go out to the airstrip and set up the cones." They ran out of the kitchen and seemed to know exactly what to do, as if they had done it many times before. The boys barely put out the cones in time.

Ralph Lowen enjoyed his work with Life Lion. A former SuperCobra attack helicopter pilot with the U.S. Marine Corps, he saw combat in both the Persian Gulf War and in Operation Iraqi Freedom before retraining for civilian service.

This call made him wish his Life Lion aircraft could move as swiftly as his military choppers in previous years. Even his fellow crew members were more tense than usual, and that was saying something for such a veteran medical trauma team.

They all were relieved when they saw the telltale airstrip off of County Road 641 near Newburg, Pennsylvania. In no mood to lose any more time, Lowen quickly spiraled down in an abrupt military-style landing near some orange cones apparently set out by two waiting boys standing at the edge of the airstrip.

The surprise landing left his companions a little breathless, but they clearly were relieved to finally land so they could find this hurting boy.

When Lowen cut power to the rotors, his trauma crew hit the ground with gear in hand even before the rotors had stopped their rotation. With barely a nod, the two boys spun on their heels and bolted for a nearby farmhouse as fast as their legs could take them. Clearly their minds were focused on something or someone in that house.

The trauma team didn't need any more information. Since the ambulance wasn't waiting for them yet, they knew they had made good time. The crew decided to walk the distance to the house for an early look at their patient so they could be better prepared to care for him once they were in the air.

The Life Lion crew followed the boys directly into the kitchen without knocking or offering formal introductions—they weren't needed. It was clear that everyone in that crowded kitchen was relieved they had come so quickly. The local EMTs were still getting the young boy ready for transport when they walked in. (This was yet another miracle in Trevor's amazing journey from tragedy to triumph.)

When the Life Lion team walked in with their trademark uniforms and equipment, Troy felt a lump rise in his throat. *This will be Trevor's second helicopter ride, he mused. I can still remember the time a Life Lion crew came to little two-year-old Trevor's hospital room.* He was suffering from a life-threatening case of croup, and they came to the small local hospital to fly him to a larger regional medical center for more specialized care.

Now Trevor was going to fly again.

"Trevor," Troy said, trying to keep the tremor out of his voice, "I hope this is the *last* helicopter ride of this kind you will ever have to take."

Trevor tried to smile, but within a few seconds he began to close his eyes. Immediately, one of the medics leaned closer and said, "Trevor, stay with us, son. You need to stay awake for a little while. Okay?"

The other medic quietly explained to Troy and Debbie that they wanted Trevor to stay awake to help ward off shock. When he noticed that Trevor was fighting to hold his eyes open, he decided to try a joke.

"What did the bartender say when the horse walked in?" the medic said as he watched for a response.

Trevor wasn't used to jokes because his family didn't tell many. As with so many families tracing their history to Mennonite and Amish ancestors who came to America for religious freedom, telling jokes just wasn't a normal part of their lives. They were so busy working and playing hard as a family that they didn't have much leisure time. The time they did have they spent together as a family.

Unsure how to respond, Trevor just looked up at the medic and said nothing. Determined to deliver the punch line to his joke, the medic pressed on despite the deafening silence from his young audience:

"He asked the horse, '*Why is your face so long?*'" the medic answered with a smile. "That was the only dumb joke I know. I know it wasn't very good."

At that point, Trevor mustered a weak laugh anyway, and Troy realized that was the whole point. The medic wanted to draw Trevor's attention away from his injuries and help him relax and laugh a little.

When Troy glanced across the kitchen island at Debbie, he noticed she was smiling, too. She felt encouraged by Trevor's laughter as well. *If you want to get Trevor to laugh, tell a joke with a farm animal in it somewhere,* he mused. *That boy loves animals.*

One of the most curious and astounding things Troy noticed from the earliest moment Trevor was conscious after the accident became very noticeable in the kitchen: Despite his horrific injuries, Trevor never complained of any pain.

Whether it was Troy or one of the medics, whenever someone asked, "Are you hurting anywhere, son?" Trevor would calmly say, "No."

Amazing. That was the only word for it. But was Trevor's nervous system temporarily put "on hold" or suspended in some way due to a mystery of the human body when faced with trauma? Only time would tell.

Even the medical personnel in that kitchen seemed to be baffled and relieved. They all had experienced the searing emotions of pain gone amuck in serious accident victims. It was an experience no one should have to endure or witness.

Once the EMTs completed their preparations to help stabilize Trevor during transport, they carefully moved him through the kitchen door and into the waiting ambulance. From there they drove him from the house to the waiting helicopter on the airstrip. Troy followed the ambulance while Debbie remained with the younger children in the farmhouse.

As much as she wanted to be at Trevor's side every step of the journey ahead, she was very aware of her other children and how difficult this crisis was for them.

It only took a few minutes for the ambulance to pull up beside the sleek Life Lion 2 medivac helicopter, and at that point the trauma crew officially assumed responsibility for Trevor's care. Then, both crews worked together to quickly transfer him from the ambulance to the helicopter.

As the flight crew began to secure Trevor for air transport, Troy asked the pilot, "Can I ride with him?"

"No, I'm sorry," Lowen told him, his voice full of sympathy. "It's a hospital policy and a matter of insurance and liability. I'm really sorry. I think I'd ask the same question."

Determined not to delay Trevor's journey to the trauma center even one more minute, Troy kissed his son tenderly on the forehead.

"Daddy and Mommy will be down later," he said, trying to sound cheerful. "You just go on with them and they'll take good care of you. They'll get you all wrapped up."

Then the hatch closed, the engines started, and the massive rotors began to rotate overhead.

Troy stood on that lonely airstrip, feeling helpless and anxious as he watched the helicopter whisk away Trevor. In the eerie silence after the beat of the helicopter rotors faded in the distance, Troy put words to the agony in his soul, wondering, *O God, what is going to happen to my son? Will I ever get to see that little boy alive again?*

Troy and Debbie were anxious to get on the road and follow the helicopter to the Penn State Hershey Medical Center, but they had to wait. It wasn't easy, but they had no choice—every farmer in the area knew that serious farm accidents had to be officially investigated by the Pennsylvania State Police.

Considering the nature of Trevor's accident and the extent of his injuries, they knew the police would want to conduct a thorough investigation.

It may sound odd to people who don't live in agricultural areas, but farm accidents are treated somewhat like automobile accidents. Investigation files are official documents useful in court cases involving medical claims or liability lawsuits. State farm bureaus and university agricultural institutes also use them to track accidents involving farm crews and heavy equipment. Their updated safety guidelines have saved many lives, and they often encourage manufacturers to install better safety shields and modify equipment for better worker safety.

Troy and Debbie knew the State Police investigator was on his way because he was notified by the 9-1-1 operator at the same time as the emergency medical personnel. In the meantime, Troy noticed that his two oldest boys had seemed to disappear once Trevor was taken to the airstrip.

When he finally found them in the barn, they were sitting on a rafter in the hayloft just staring into space. Trent already had parked the uniloader in the barn and dumped the contents of the bucket—the debris spit out of the harvester chute—in a pile.

He could sense something was wrong with them. *Those boys are feeling the heavy weight of guilt,* he thought. *They are trying to blame themselves for Trevor's accident.*

He knew he had to do something to jolt them out of that self-destructive thinking track. "Boys!" he said gruffly. "You need to get ready ... right now!"

They dropped to the ground immediately, ready to obey even before they knew what they were to get ready for. "Dad, what do you want us to do? Where are we going?"

"You need to go with me and your mother. We have to leave soon so we can be there with Trevor and help him pull through this."

Relief seemed to flood across their faces. He couldn't have made it any clearer that he didn't blame them for the accident; instead, he wanted them right there at Trevor's side as part of his recovery team. Troy suspected his idea had worked when they rushed past him in a mad race to see who would reach the kitchen door first.

He looked at the pile of silage intermingled with shreds of clothing that had been dumped on the ground and suddenly felt the urge to sort through it. His effort was rewarded when he found Trevor's second shoe that had been hidden in the debris.

Troy trudged wearily back to the kitchen door and took one last glance at the barn and at the deserted airstrip before going inside.

As he passed through the kitchen, he noticed that Debbie had carefully set aside Trevor's bloody shirt and jacket and bundled them with his mangled pants and shoes recovered from the accident site.

Troy was thinking how much he needed a shower to wash away the evidence of his worst day when a Pennsylvania State Police cruiser pulled up to the house. Things had moved quickly since the accident, but to the Beams it seemed an eternity had passed.

Fortunately, the officer was sensitive to their situation. He carefully took their official statements and jotted down the basic facts of the accident. Then he looked up from his report file with a smile and said, "You don't belong here. *Get going!*"

With a great feeling of relief, Troy walked the officer to the door. As soon as the door was shut, he peeled off the bloody shirt he was wearing when he carried Trevor from the harvester wagon to the kitchen and put it in the bag with Trevor's clothes from the accident. Then he remembered the missing shirt sleeve and quickly retrieved it from his office doorway. *Maybe the day will come when the memories attached to these clothes will be more useful than painful,* he thought to himself.

His mind was a blur of back-to-back memories as he stumbled mechanically into the shower to wash off the blood and prepare for the drive to Hershey. It only took him five minutes to shower, but Debbie already had a fresh shirt and a pair of jeans waiting for him. As he dressed, Debbie told him that his parents had volunteered to watch

Tiffany and the younger kids while they made their emergency drive to Hershey.

He was amazed at Debbie's ability to manage and arrange everything in the household while carrying such an emotional weight herself. But the pinched expression on Debbie's face told him her mind was already an hour away with her critically injured little boy in Hershey, Pennsylvania.

Troy sent T.J. and Trent on one last quick circuit of the house and farmyard to check all of the doors, gates, and water and feed troughs. Then all four of them climbed into the truck and headed for the highway.

"It was so good of your parents to take our four youngest children, especially with your dad not feeling well," Debbie said with a sigh. "There's no telling how long we'll be at the hospital."

With the peaceful scene of the farm in the rearview mirror, Troy sensed they were driving into an emotional firestorm that would test the depths of their faith and character.

Glancing at Debbie to his right and at the boys in the back of the crew cab, Troy said, "'Let's pray for Trevor right now. He needs nothing less than a miracle, so we need to pray like we've never prayed before."

"God, help that little boy!"

CHAPTER THREE

"WE NEED YOUR PERMISSION TO REMOVE TREVOR'S LEG"

Four people huddled in the truck cab as it hurtled past farm after farm in the Pennsylvania countryside. They were oblivious to everything but their destination.

The tense drive from the farm to the Children's Hospital at the Penn State Hershey Medical Center took a little over an hour, and the four appeared to pass the time in quiet conversation and prayer. Yet, each of them felt as if that brief 60-minute journey was a 60-hour endurance contest spent in the world's slowest moving vehicle.

Troy and Debbie had no idea how Trevor was doing; the evidence available when they last saw him aboard the Life Lion helicopter provided very little hope. They only could entrust their son's life to the Lord, just as they always had done.

"O God, please help our son. Surround him with Your presence and be near him. We need You so very much, Lord."

When they finally drove onto the medical campus in Hershey, the early afternoon sun in Pennsylvania's winter season was glistening on the snow-covered ground. They glanced at all of the buildings, but their eyes were riveted by the telltale orange windsock blowing in the breeze at the Life Lion heliport.

One by one, they each secretly imagined the scene when Trevor arrived at that landing pad just a few hours earlier, only to be whisked away into one of those nearby buildings.

Debbie pulled her gaze away from the heliport to look at the cluster of imposing hospital buildings. She felt a little intimidated by the sheer mass and size of the campus.

Shivering instinctively, she couldn't repress the passing thought that had invaded her mind over and over again in the quiet interior of the truck. *Will we ever leave this place with Trevor and have a normal life again?*

The four family members pulled their coat collars closer against the penetrating winter cold and walked stiffly in a clustered group through automatic doors and up to the counter in the Emergency Room.

When Troy asked about Trevor, the lady at the tall counter looked at her computer screen for what seemed like a half hour before looking over her glasses and saying, "I'm sorry, sir, but we have *no record* of any Trevor Beam being admitted for treatment. Are you sure that happened *today?*"

It would have been a great opportunity to panic, but Troy persisted. Patiently, he explained that Trevor had *just come in* on a Life Lion flight. It seemed reasonable to him that even Penn State Hershey didn't have *that* many helicopter trauma arrivals in one day.

Sure enough, after some additional inquiries by phone, the receptionist finally located Trevor somewhere in the bowels of the hospital.

"It turns out you are right, Mr. Beam," the receptionist said. "Trevor *is* here, but he is still being examined by the trauma team assigned to his case. Someone from trauma will come to see you as soon as he can. You can wait for the doctor right there, in the trauma waiting area."

Troy, Debbie, and the boys were expecting to hear a status report on Trevor when they walked through the doora. The word *wait* just wasn't on their "most popular word" list. It was about to drop to the bottom of that list because, as they discovered, it was evidently the most popular word in the medical vocabulary.

It seemed that things had moved so quickly—including the rapid transit of the Beam family from Cumberland County to Hershey, Pennsylvania—that no one was ready to tell them anything about Trevor.

Their only comforting thought at that moment was that somewhere in that building a team of top medical specialists and support personnel were hovering over Trevor. If they were slow to communicate with the family, it was only because they were so determined to evaluate the extent of Trevor's injuries and form a battle plan to save his life and help him heal from the wounds of his horrendous accident.

It took all the four waiting Beams had to fight back the constant barrage of negative thoughts and unthinkable outcomes bombarding their minds. Later, they discovered that, one by one, each of them had struggled to guard their thoughts and keep hope alive while secretly fearing the worst.

The agony of *simply not knowing* continued without any relief for several hours while they waited for someone ... *anyone* ... to tell them what was going on with Trevor.

Finally the elevator doors opened and someone in surgical scrubs stepped out and walked over to them. As he approached, the family stood up while trying desperately to hide any trace of dread from their faces.

"How is he?" Troy asked.

"Considering the nature and extent of his injuries, Trevor is doing remarkably well," the doctor replied. "We're still stabilizing him and making sure that all the life-threatening elements of his injuries are under control, but he is holding his own. The primary physician will be down shortly to give you a fuller assessment."

With collective sighs of relief, all four of them plopped back into their seats as soon as the doctor disappeared into the elevator once again. A few minutes later another man dressed in similar scrubs entered the waiting area.

He walked in with a smile, quickly scanned their anxious faces, and then said quietly, gently, with a hint of a British accent:

"I'm Doctor Boustred. I'm a specialist in plastic surgery and I'm the primary doctor leading the team that is taking care of Trevor.

"I'm sure you have heard the preliminary report. Trevor is now stabilized and is doing as well as can be expected.

"It looks like we'll be able to save Trevor's left leg..." the doctor hesitated briefly before continuing, *"but probably not his right."*

He could see the devastating effect of his words on the parents, and he hurried to explain as well as he could.

"The damage is too severe. As I'm sure you already know, *his right calf muscle was filleted from the bone, just as you would fillet a fish, and part of it was hanging down at his ankle. In addition, two of the three main blood vessels to his foot have been ripped out and the third is damaged.* He also has suffered nerve damage to his foot."

Words like these were so difficult to say; he was a father himself. Physician or not, he prayed he would never hear what he had to say to this precious family on that cold January night.

"Amputate?" Troy asked with a sick feeling in his stomach. He glanced at Debbie, whose face mirrored the fear in his own heart. Then he looked back at the doctor. "Is there no other way?"

"I understand this is a big blow to you," the doctor said, his eyes full of sympathy for the distraught parents before him. "But it's truly amazing what they can do with prosthetics these days. Children in particular do quite well. At his age, Trevor will have no trouble adapting to an artificial limb."

T.J. and Trent looked soberly at each other. *Prosthetics? Artificial limbs? What were those things?* These were new terms to the boys, but judging by the anguish in their parents' eyes, they knew Mom and Dad didn't want those things for Trevor.

"But Trevor always has been so athletic," Troy said. "He's one of the most athletic of our boys. I can't bear the thought of him being so damaged for life."

"Don't worry," the doctor assured them. "Once Trevor is fitted for an artificial leg and gets used to it, he will run and play football again like he did before. In fact, it will seem as though he has no prosthesis at all."

Troy was still mulling this over when the doctor added something more.

"There's another problem with the right foot that makes it virtually impossible to save it. Because of the damage to the blood vessels, *Trevor has no blood going to his right foot. Without blood circulation, his foot will die.*"

Debbie suddenly spoke up to ask, "Has his foot lost color?"

"No, and that's what we don't understand. We can't find a pulse in Trevor's foot, which means no blood flow. Normally, his foot should be chalky white under this condition, but it isn't; it is still pink.

"I can't explain it, but I can tell you this: Even if Trevor keeps his leg, without blood flow he will never be able to use his foot again. *The only thing Trevor has remaining on his right leg is a strip about an inch wide down the front. Everything else has been ripped off.*"

Another man in surgical scrubs quietly joined the group in the waiting area during the conversation and politely interjected himself into the discussion right at the end.

"Hi, I'm Doctor Goslein, the vascular surgeon who will be working on Trevor's legs. I have to reinforce what Doctor Boustred said. I've never tried to put blood vessels into the leg of anyone as young as Trevor. Generally, they are too small and they usually don't work because they collapse so easily."

Troy and Debbie could feel the invisible weight of hopelessness pressing on them with crushing force. For a moment, they were totally speechless. They were doing their best to take it all in, but the sheer shock of the day's events was overwhelming.

The day had begun so peacefully, so very normally. Then, in a moment's time, Trevor was nearly killed right in their own farmyard. And here they were, seemingly just a short time later, calmly discussing Trevor's life *without* a leg, along with nerve damage, prosthetics, and who knows what else to come.

The word *shock* was too weak and shallow to describe the way they felt in that moment. This simply was not what they had hoped to hear.

The primary doctor noticed the conspicuous silence after his briefing, so he nervously continued in hopes that the shocked parents in front of him would agree to cooperate with their plan of medical treatment.

"What you need to understand, Mr. and Mrs. Beam, is that *even if Trevor keeps his leg, he probably will never be able to walk on it again.* The damage is simply too severe.

"The only possibility, and it is remote at best, would be to take some muscle tissue from Trevor's back and try to graft it onto his leg. It would be extremely painful for him.

"He would have to wear a brace and probably would have trouble with it for the rest of his life."

Debbie gazed silently into Troy's eyes for a few moments and shook her head slightly. Then Troy said, "We understand what you're saying, Doctor, and we appreciate your candor and your honesty. But we just don't know."

The doctor paused for a moment before pressing in with an even more direct message.

"Mr. Beam, all I need you to do is sign this paper here, *we need your permission to remove Trevor's leg.* We'll try to save it below the knee, but because some of the damage extends above the knee, we may have to take it off above the knee."

Throughout this conversation Troy had been praying silently, seeking God's direction in their desperate situation. What was best for Trevor?

He knew from the apostle Paul's instruction to Christians facing hard decisions in the first century that *peace* was one of the things God uses to guide His people through difficult passages in life. He said, *"And let the **peace of God** rule in your hearts, to the which also ye are called in one body; and be ye thankful."* [1]

Silently, he breathed a prayer even while the doctors looked for their response. *Lord, what do You want?*

When Troy looked at Debbie, he still could see the lingering remnants of fear and grief etched across the contours of her lovely face, but he saw something else, too. It was visible in her eyes.

He saw confidence. It was as if Debbie was saying to him in unspoken words, *"Whatever you decide, I'm with you. We are all in this together."* When he glanced at the boys, it was clear that they felt even more overwhelmed by the doctors' reports, but they also were looking to their father with confidence.

Finally, Troy sensed he had the answer for that particular moment, and that was all he needed. Turning his head away from Debbie and the boys, Troy looked directly into the primary doctor's eyes and said with clear determination:

"Taking off Trevor's leg is not an option. I have more faith in God than that. I *know* that God can heal his leg, and I at least want to give Him the chance to do so."

Troy felt Debbie's hand squeeze his. Secretly her heart swelled with pride at his intestinal fortitude. *He has more guts than any man in the world!* she thought to herself.

The doctor looked at them for several seconds while carefully pondering his response. "Well, I'm a Christian, too," he said finally. "I, too, believe that God can heal, but I also know that God does not always answer our prayers the way we would like."

Again, the doctor paused as though he was carefully weighing his next words. "However," he continued, "if you want me to try to put Trevor's leg back together, then I would like to have prayer with you right here."

"Absolutely!" Troy said without hesitation.

Troy and Debbie knelt down with the two doctors in that small waiting room as the boys bowed their heads in silent agreement. Together, they took the terrible weight of Trevor's crisis to the One who created him and held his future in His hand. The Bible tells us to humble ourselves under God's hand, *"...casting all your care upon him; for he careth for you."* [2]

Dr. Boustred, Trevor's primary physician, prayed first.

"Lord, naturally speaking, this looks impossible. But if this father wants us to try to put this leg together, then we're going to need Your wisdom, Your guidance, and Your help."

Then Troy prayed a prayer he had never prayed before, and one he hoped he never would pray again.

"Lord, please guide these good doctors as they work on Trevor's leg. Guide their hands and help them use their best skills as they operate on our son.

"Father, You are the Great Physician, and nothing is impossible for You. I ask You please to heal Trevor, in Jesus' name, amen."

Debbie tried unsuccessfully to stop the flood of tears flowing down her face as she silently agreed with her husband's prayer. Only the Lord could understand the fierce intensity and power of her fervent prayer, rising from the depths of a mother's love for her son.

Just before the doctors turned to take the elevator back to the surgical suite, Troy said, "Doctor, if it will help, I'll gladly donate some of my blood vessels or muscle tissue—I'll give you whatever is needed."

Dr. Boustred smiled and hurriedly answered as the elevator doors closed, "Thank you for the offer, but it wouldn't work. Trevor's body would reject them. We have to use his tissue."

The doctors went back up for the surgery while Troy, Debbie, and the boys sat down again to continue their anxious wait.

There wasn't much for them to do except talk and pray. Trevor's future seemed to be totally out of their hands. Their minds swirled with questions and thoughts.

Troy broke an awkward silence early in the wait, mentioning to Debbie and the boys, "Gathering from their conversation, those doctors seem to be pretty certain that Trevor is going to live. *Thank You, Lord!*"

As they already had discovered, even good news can trigger new fears about potentially bad news to follow. As soon as they began to thank God for His faithfulness in saving Trevor's life, their minds were deluged with questions about the *quality* of that life.

- If Trevor survives this accident, what happens then?

- What if the surgery fails?

- What if Trevor's leg really is damaged too severely to be repaired?

- Will he end up losing his leg after all?

- Will he be crippled for the rest of his life?

- Yes, God *could* heal Trevor, but what if He chose not to? What then?

They didn't know it at the time, but their tense vigil would drag on for five-and-a-half more hours that night.

Troy and the boys read every dog-eared sports and automotive magazine they could find in the waiting area—and they even briefly thought about reading some of the "ladies' magazines" out of desperation.

Debbie read some magazines, but she also could describe in detail every piece of furniture and each children's toy that was stationed in the waiting area.

One after the other, she imagined boys and girls playing with those toys in relative innocence while their parents sat in those chairs and wrestled with some of the most life-threatening and heart-wrenching questions of human existence. *And she was one of them.* No one had *asked* her to do it; she never had *expected* it. But here she was, asking God for miracle after miracle.

She was thankful for childish innocence and for the fact that her little ones did not comprehend the pain or agony that Trevor and their parents might be going through that day. She desperately longed for a normal day again, like the hundreds of days she had enjoyed—and taken for granted—before the accident.

The cycle of fighting off despair and waiting numbly counterbalanced by moments of soaring hope and fervent prayer seemed endless.

But the moment finally came when the elevator door opened and Dr. Boustred walked out to speak with them, still wearing his operating room scrubs with his mask hanging below his chin.

Troy noticed the mask and the surgical "socks" still covering the surgeon's street shoes and understood that he had come down directly from surgery rather than taking time to change. He thought to himself, *This man didn't waste any time getting down here to fill us in. Thank You, Lord, for a doctor who understands our need to know something—anything—about the well-being of our little boy.*

"We just wheeled Trevor out of the operating room...everything looks okay so far."

The doctor and the four family members started for the PICU [Pediatric Intensive Care Unit] to see Trevor. At that point, Troy and the boys all noticed how Debbie's eyes seemed to light up with fresh hope. Then Dr. Boustred continued his report.

"We transplanted blood vessels from his upper left leg and put his calf muscle back together with the new vessels. Finally, we sewed up his leg and packed it in a sterile dressing.

"At this point, we'll simply have to wait and see what happens. But you should know that *if the condition of his leg becomes life-threatening to Trevor*, we may have to take it off quickly, even without your permission."

"I don't want to threaten his life," Troy replied, relieved at the encouraging report. "We understand that you have to do what you have to do, but in the meantime we are going to pray that God will give him a healing touch."

"We won't open the dressing on Trevor's leg again until Saturday," Dr. Boustred said. "That allows us to get a clear picture of how much of his leg will live. If things look good, that is the time we will take muscle tissue from his back and graft it onto his leg."

"How will that affect Trevor?" Troy asked. "Will he be bent over for the rest of his life?"

"No. His back will feel sore and weak for awhile, but it will strengthen up once again."

"So what's next?" Troy asked.

"On Saturday evening we'll take Trevor back to the operating room, open the dressing on his leg, clean it up, and cut away any muscle or other tissue that has died in the meantime. The last thing we want is for dead tissue to remain because it's a breeding place for bacteria and infection. And you certainly know as well as anyone that farm accidents in particular are exceptionally prone to infection."

"Is there anything else we can do?"

"Not tonight. Trevor is still pretty well out of it from the anesthesia and nothing more is planned in his treatment until Saturday. If you'd like, you may see him in his room for a few minutes. Then you may as well go home and try to get some rest. You've had a busy Thursday!"

Troy instinctively extended his hand to his son's doctor and said with heartfelt sincerity, "Thanks, Doctor Boustred. That little boy means all the world to us. I don't think it was a coincidence that you and your team were on duty ... when Trevor arrived. We appreciate all you've done and all you are doing for him. God bless you! Good night."

A night shift nurse looked up as the surgeon quietly slipped into an elevator, and then she glanced at the family of four obviously huddled together in prayer near the elevator.

She had seen a lot of people pray in that hospital. Since it was a teaching hospital with specialized services for the most serious of injuries and childhood diseases, she had seen a lot of desperation in her years of service.

47

Yet, there seemed to be something special about that family. As the four of them stepped onto the elevator and disappeared, her curiosity led her to check the day logs. Beam… *Trevor Beam*. She would remember that name and add this boy to her own prayer list. Perhaps she would meet this young patient soon.

After a short time with their unconcious son, Troy, Debbie, and the boys left the hospital and walked the hundred yards or so across the frozen parking lot to the truck, shivering in the cold winter wind. They made the journey to this place burdened by one type of concern. Now they would return home with thanksgiving, but carrying yet *another* set of concerns for Trevor.

At last they arrived at the darkened farmhouse. The four wearily dragged themselves inside to fall into their beds, emotionally and physically exhausted.

Several hours later in the early morning darkness, Troy lay awake, unable to fall back to sleep. He thought of his young son an hour away from home in a strange hospital bed, mangled horribly, his future uncertain. He fought the crushing waves of mental anguish that threatened to overcome his mind with a despair stronger than he ever had felt in his life. Debbie woke up a short while later, shivering uncontrollably.

"Troy," she said softly, her voice trembling, "I just can't take this! I don't know what to do." She began to weep so violently that he could feel the bed shaking beneath him.

Troy rolled toward her and wrapped her in his arms. Softly he spoke in a pleading voice, "Honey, don't do this to me! I can't take it either. Let's pray. Let's ask God to give us peace."

They bowed their heads together in silence for a moment, his big hands stroking her long, brown hair in the darkness. Then Troy prayed, "Lord, we don't know what to do. Please take away this fear and give us Your peace."

That was enough. With a gentle kiss on her cheek and a reassuring hug, they both went back to sleep and slept soundly until morning.

An hour's drive away, Trevor lay in an anesthesia-induced sleep with his right leg completely engulfed in a large white dressing and his left nearly covered in bandages as well. Several tubes and a bulky monitor line assembly crisscrossed his bed as lights and LEDs blinked constantly, tracking every vital sign in the little boy's severely damaged body.

Nearly every 30 minutes, it seemed, a nurse silently whisked into his PICU room to verify the readings on his monitoring systems. The real reason was even more important: She knew there was no substitute for the practiced eye and trained instincts of a caring nurse.

She couldn't rest until she knew this little boy had a fighting chance. Only after she had double-checked every monitor line and IV line and manually checked Trevor's pulse and blood pressure would she slowly back out of his room. It was almost as if she couldn't take her eyes off of him. *If this keeps up, I'll never be able to take care of my other patients,* she thought to herself as she reluctantly closed the glass door behind her.

Endnotes

1. Colossians 3:15. The *Amplified Version* of the Bible, which helps reveal the full meanings of the original languages used in Bible manuscripts, puts it this way: *"And let the peace (soul harmony which comes) from Christ rule (act as umpire continually) in your hearts [deciding and settling with finality all questions that arise in your minds, in that peaceful state] to which as [members of Christ's] one body you were also called [to live]. And be thankful (appreciative), [giving praise to God always]"* (Colossians 3:15, AMP).

2. See First Peter 5:6-7.

Chapter Four

"Trevor Is My Son, Too"

Friday dawned as a fast-paced day for the Beam family following a long night with little sleep. The older family members tackled their duties with Trevor on their minds.

Even in a time of crisis, there were still animals to feed, farm chores to complete, and for Troy, an expanding construction company to run. Yet, Trevor remained foremost in his mind. As he fielded the regular business phone calls, his mind was preoccupied with questions for Trevor's well-being. His heart yearned for his young son and many times throughout that long day he found himself staring at his desk full of paperwork, unable to see anything but a small boy lying atop a wagon's beaters. It would take a long time for that awful memory to fade.

Finally, late in the afternoon, Troy and Debbie loaded the children into the family van and drove back to the hospital to visit Trevor. Forthe length of the drive and throughout the day Friday, their thoughts kept returning to the crucial events the doctors had scheduled for Saturday.

Just before they left the house, Troy called certain people he knew who were strong Christians and asked them to pray for the healing of Trevor's leg. He and Debbie also called family members in Pennsylvania, Ohio, and Indiana with an update on Trevor.

Both partners already held strong personal beliefs in the power of prayer. However, Troy and Debbie sensed they would experience it in a tangible way as never before during Trevor's hospitalization and recovery.

The news of Trevor's accident had spread quickly through the many close-knit communities in their region, particularly among the area churches. As a result, united prayer began to increase on an unprecedented level.

The outpouring of love that the family received almost was overwhelming. Cards, e-mails, and gifts began to arrive from all around the region and even from other states. Hope and encouragement are vital to the healing process, and the outpouring of love and support from friends and strangers alike brought much hope and encouragement to Trevor and the family.

Yet, on this Friday, only one day away from one of Trevor's most crucial decision points, Troy and Debbie had many questions and uncertainties but very little good news to hold on to. So they held on to one another ... and to God.

They made a rapid trip to Hershey that afternoon knowing they would have to come right back home again late that night, only to return the next morning.

After all, *this was Trevor,* and *he needed them.* They canceled previous plans and made new arrangements just for the opportunity to see their son for a brief period that night. It was worth it all, even though they suspected Trevor still would be too heavily sedated to know they were there.

The doctors told them they planned to keep Trevor in an unconscious state, assuming he would be in excruciating pain if he woke up. They also were worried that he might move or thrash around and endanger any potential healing that might take place in his severely damaged right leg.

Although Trevor was in the PICU [Pediatric Intensive Care Unit], the doctors allowed Troy and Debbie to bring the children into Trevor's room.

From the instant they filed into Trevor's room, Debbie just couldn't pull her eyes away from her son's swollen face.

Her heart brimmed over with gratitude for the doctor's successful bid to save her son's life, but it also broke every time she saw her little boy strapped to a bed with the breathing tube down his throat, the chest drainage tube, the PICC line attached to the IV bag, a full array of electronic sensors, and his elaborate patchwork of bandages.

Later, the nurses told her that Trevor was given medication to make him *forget* a lot of the early hospital stay, and *she* began to wonder if she needed to forget these early days at the hospital as well!

She looked across Trevor's bed to her husband and spoke softly between nearly silent sobs.

"Troy, when I first saw Trevor lying here, I was afraid I would pass out. Honestly, he seemed almost dead. I couldn't stand watching his chest rise and fall in rhythm with that breathing machine.

"I know the doctors are afraid he will hurt himself in his sleep, but it is so hard to see him lying there with his hands tied to the bed rails.

"Trevor is so out of it today. His eyes look so shiny and puffy; and it hurts me to look at his legs—all wrapped up from toes to groin."

Troy nodded and quickly looked away to wipe away a tear before taking Trevor's delicate fingers in his own work-hardened hands. Then Debbie leaned over the bed rail and whispered softly into Trevor's ear:

"Trevor, Daddy and Mommy are here. We love you. You're our buddy." (Troy always called his boys "buddies".)

"It won't be long and you'll be all better again. God's gonna watch over you, too."

It seemed so strange to leave her son in someone else's care as their "patient." Something deep inside her, something instinctual and emotional to the core, was crying out in silent waves of frustration, "He is *my* son—not *your* patient!"

Surprised at her own reaction, Debbie thought to herself, *The truth is that I'm deeply grateful for all of the wonderful care these men and women give my son, but it is obvious that my mother's heart also carries an unreasoning jealousy, small though it may be.*

She carefully walked around Trevor's bed and all of the machinery that seemed to encircle him and looked at Troy.

"Troy, I just want to hold him in my arms and tell him it's going to be okay. But here we are, totally helpless and unable to do anything but pray.

"It's hard, but we have no choice except to relinquish his care to complete strangers.

"How long will we have to talk to Trevor in this drugged state? I just want to hear his voice again...."

Troy nodded and began to softly sing to Trevor, and Debbie joined in. They had done it ever since Trevor was born.

After some time, Trevor gradually awoke from his induced sleep. As Troy and Debbie leaned forward, tears spilled from Trevor's swollen eyes and he seemed as if he was pleading for something.

Desperate to comfort him, but knowing he could not speak with the breathing tube in his mouth, they rubbed his forehead, held his hand, and strained to understand him as their hearts silently broke.

Over and over again, Trevor tried desperately to say something, and his parents did their best to understand him. "Say it again, please, Trevor." So each time, he would fix his expressive blue eyes on their faces, looking first at one and then the other, trying to form words around the breathing tube taped to his mouth.

His lips were peeling as if they were terribly dry and dehydrated. Then Troy figured it out. "That's it! Thirsty. Are you thirsty, Trevor?" When Trevor nodded slightly, Troy said, "He wants a drink! Call the nurse."

Unfortunately, the staff couldn't remove the breathing tube, so Trevor couldn't swallow any liquids. However, the nurse hurried back with a tiny sponge so they could dip it in water and moisten his lips. That seemed to satisfy Trevor, and he lay back in his bed once more.

Debbie and Troy moved closer to his bed and said, "Trevor, do you know that Tiffany is here?"

Immediately, Trevor nodded his head "yes" and tried to extend his hand, which was strapped to the rail, toward his twin sister.

"Do you want to hold her hand?" Troy asked.

When Trevor again nodded his head "yes," Tiffany couldn't wait any longer. She quickly clasped his hand in her own, and it was almost all Debbie could handle.

The bittersweet picture of her precious son battling for his life and limb surrounded by tubes and machines in that PICU room while holding hands with his twin sister was heart-wrenching.

And yet, it also brought her comfort. She knew that brief moment shared with Tiffany just might do as much for Trevor's little fighting spirit as all of the drugs in the world. If *anybody* could encourage Trevor, it would be Tiffany.

After they had visited with Trevor for awhile, the doctors ordered him sedated again and the family prayed over him. With feelings of relief, sadness, and the weight of the unknown, Troy, Debbie, and the children quietly walked back to the van, hand in hand, for the trip home.

All was quiet when they finally drove back up the lane to their home in the dark of night, and neither Troy nor Debbie could go to sleep immediately. There was much to pray about.

Saturday morning finally came.

Troy rolled out of bed long before the sun rose with one thought dominating all others in his mind: *This is the big day.* In just a matter of hours, that very *evening* in fact, the doctors would open up Trevor's leg and determine what would happen next.

Either they would move forward with further surgery and treatment or *they would amputate Trevor's leg* if too much muscle tissue had died.

It was just as simple and as heartbreaking as that.

Once again, the Beam family went through the demanding routines of running a farm and operating the thriving construction business, looking forward to the moment they could climb in the truck and drive eastward for Hershey.

Despite the hectic work pace, the hours seemed to creep by as they awaited the evening procedure. At one point that day, Troy walked into the boys' bedroom and felt a stab of nostalgia in his heart as his mind was flooded with waves of vivid memories.

I grew up in this house, he thought to himself, wiping away a tear. *In fact, this was my room, too.*

Memories and treasured associations from the past can make certain things and places special to us, and that room was special to Troy. Suddenly, he felt overwhelmed by emotion and grief for his young son. He knelt beside a little white chair in the room and began to cry out to God.

"Lord, I've heard of miracles You've done in our day. I know You have healed people because I've heard their testimonies.

"If there is one time in my life that You will let me personally see a miracle, please let me see one this time. Please heal Trevor's leg."

As he continued to pray for Trevor's healing, Troy suddenly felt God's presence overshadow him. And he could actually sense the Lord was speaking into his spirit. He didn't hear an audible voice, but he felt the Lord's presence. A sensation of deep comfort seemed to settle into his heart. He felt he could hear his Father in heaven speaking to his spirit.

"Trevor is My son, too. I am going to take good care of him."

Troy was so stunned by the Lord's words that he simply quit praying. What else could he say? He bowed his head and sat in stillness and reverential awe. Minute by minute, he just basked in the Lord's presence without a word. He could feel peace and courage rise inside of him even as he faced one of the most difficult times in his life.

Troy remained in that kneeling position of prayer, quietly enjoying the warm glow of His Father's presence, until he heard Debbie say with alarm, "Where's the fire?"

Instantly, Troy was jerked back into the realm of the ordinary and he jumped to his feet, moving toward the door even as he called out, "Fire? What's burning?"

He was about halfway across the room and heading for the door when he felt that extraordinary sense of the Lord's presence leaving him. The word *fire* just kept pounding at his will with urgency, demanding his total attention. But Troy had just experienced something he desperately needed in this crisis with Trevor. He abruptly turned back from the door and spoke out his heart's desire:

"Lord, don't leave me; I'm not done. I don't want to lose this sense of communion, of our sweet fellowship.

"I don't care what's on fire; Debbie and T.J. can take care of it. You know what it is. I'm not done talking with You."

Then Troy fell to his knees once more, overwhelmed with the strong emotions welling up inside. He sensed that his feelings were more than mere emotional responses to stress. No, they were his feeble attempts to comprehend and cope with the sheer love of God poured out upon his pain.

"Lord, if Trevor is Your son, if You allowed this accident to happen and You're going to take care of him; then You're going to have to help this earthly father right now. Because I feel completely helpless.

"I feel devastated. I don't know what to do. You're going to have to show me if there is anything You want me to do."

Once again the sweet peace of God filled Troy's heart. When he rose to his feet again, it was with peace this time. For the first time since the accident, he was able to take care of the farm and the business the rest of the day with unbroken peace.

I'm beginning to understand what the apostle Paul meant, Troy thought to himself, *when he said God's peace—the peace that passes all understanding—would guard my heart and mind through Christ Jesus."* [1]

Ironically, Troy discovered that the "fire crisis" that nearly ended his prayer encounter prematurely was nothing more than neighbors burning leaves. And it certainly wasn't worth giving up the sweet time he had enjoyed with his heavenly Father.

Early that evening, Troy started talking to God again as he showered in preparation to visit Trevor.

"Lord, You told me that Trevor is Your son, that You allowed this to happen, and that You were going to take care of him.

"What can I do? It hurts me to know that my son is lying in that hospital bed and that he may be crippled for the rest of his life. What do You want me to do as an earthly father?"

God spoke to him again as before, planting in his mind the very words He had given to the apostle Paul as he wrote a letter to Christ's followers in ancient Philippi:

Be careful for nothing; but in every thing by prayer and supplication with thanksgiving let your requests be made known unto God (Philippians 4:6).

As Troy finished dressing, Debbie entered the room to complete her own preparations. He watched her open a drawer and said, "Honey, I feel like God just spoke to me again."

She looked up quickly and said, "What did He say?" Her eyes were bright with hope and she was thinking, *I really could use a good word from the Lord.*

This had been just as difficult for her as for Troy; she was as desperate as he was to know what was going to happen. Troy could sense that she was feeling the same pressures he had felt that morning as he answered her.

"He said we should be careful for nothing, but in every thing by prayer and supplication with thanksgiving to let our requests be made known unto Him."

Debbie looked thoughtfully at Troy for a moment before softly asking him a question.

"What is your request?"

The question hit Troy like a bucket of water. It was a good question that made him stop and think for a moment.

I know what I want, he thought, *but do I have the faith or the strength to ask?* He knew it wasn't enough simply to "want" something, even if it was a good thing. He had to make that request known to God. He had to ask.

Troy looked up toward the skylight above them and gently took Debbie's hands into his own. It was time to pray a new way.

"Lord, my wife is standing here with me, and my request to You is that You heal Trevor. I am giving my request to You, Lord, and before Debbie.

"Our request is that You heal Trevor, and that You heal him completely. Give him full use of his foot and his leg, in Your time, in Your way, for Your glory."

Debbie smiled and said in her usual matter-of-fact way, "All right, God told you to come to Him and ask, and you have." Then she added with a confidence that was obvious, "That's it; I believe it."

Well, I'm glad SHE *does,* Troy thought to himself. He still struggled to believe as he felt he should.

After all, he reasoned to himself, *it is one thing to pray and another thing to know how things will turn out in the end. God is God, after all. Even though God is always good, He often does things and answers prayers in ways we don't expect or understand.*

Through it all, he couldn't shake one question that kept rising to the top of his conscious mind every time he thought he had things calmed down. *What will they find when they open up the dressings on Trevor's leg?*

Soon it was time for yet another long drive to the hospital, but this trip somehow seemed to be even longer than the previous two trips. When Troy and Debbie finally walked into Trevor's hospital room, his bed was empty!

"Where is Trevor?" Debbie asked automatically. Troy's thoughts seemed to take on a life of their own, as if shouting the worst fears possible into an echo chamber of horrors. *Why isn't Trevor here? Are they going to come tell me he passed away now?*

Feeling stunned and in shock, Troy and Debbie looked from the empty bed to one another, and they instantly *knew* they were thinking the same horrifying thoughts and that those thoughts had *nothing* to do with faith or trust in the unfailing love that God had consistently demonstrated to them and toward Trevor. Yet, even that knowledge didn't relieve the very real distress they felt surging through them at that moment.

The lead nurse saw their facial expressions or somehow sensed that they were distraught. She was very experienced with the incredible stress of the unknown that could emotionally disable the parents of seriously ill children or, in Trevor's case, seriously injured children.

She quickly dropped her paperwork and walked directly to Troy and Debbie in Trevor's room and said, "Trevor is still in the operating room, but he will be up in just awhile." The relief on their faces reminded her that these parents needed strong reassurance that their son was still alive.

Just a few minutes later, two orderlies wheeled Trevor into the room on a gurney. He was semiconscious and still under the strong anesthesia used for the surgical procedure.

Debbie's eyes filled with tears as she looked down at Trevor in the hospital bed. She reached out to him as she said, "He looks so small and pale, Troy."

Troy looked at Trevor and quickly noticed that the doctors had removed Trevor's breathing tube in the operating room. *That is another thing to be thankful for, Lord,* he thought to himself as he looked back down the hallway to see if one of the doctors was trailing behind the gurney.

When Troy didn't see any sign of a doctor, he asked Trevor's nurse, "Where is the doctor? I want to talk to him."

"I'm sorry, Mr. Beam," the nurse said sympathetically, "but the doctor said he would be up in about a half hour to talk with you. He will fill you in on Trevor's progress then."

So once again they began playing the frustrating waiting game while their minds filled to overflowing with questions. *What would the doctor say?*

Debbie stroked Trevor's blond hair as they waited, quietly praying for him as she sought to comfort him. Her thoughts drifted back to the day she and Troy stood in a darkened room as a doctor scanned her extremely enlarged abdomen with a Doppler ultrasound unit—and announced he had found a "second ticker." Until that morning, they had no clue she was carrying twins.

On November 15th of that year, she gave birth to an 8-pound, 1-ounce boy, followed by a 7-pound, 9-ounce girl! For the next year, she and Troy struggled to care for their new twins while joking, "Half the energy and twice the work!"

Things were made worse that year because Debbie had developed back problems during the pregnancy that forced Troy to take up much of the slack as she tried to recover from the pregnancy *and* the spinal problem.

They immediately noticed there was a unique bond between Trevor and his twin sister, Tiffany. They were inseparable…and they almost seemed to coordinate their demands for eating and "other" kinds of care as well! Meanwhile, it took almost a full year for the dark circles under their parents' eyes to leave.

Troy's mind went another direction, one that was much more disturbing to him. Just two days earlier, while sitting in the waiting area waiting to learn whether Trevor would live or die that night; Troy had been tormented by feelings of guilt and regret.

As the years went by after the twins' birth, Troy noticed that he didn't have the strong connection with Trevor that he enjoyed with the other children. Something was missing, and he could see evidence of it when he looked into Trevor's blue eyes and in his attitude.

"Debbie, I just can't seem to break through with Trevor. He's a great kid, but somehow, for some reason, we just can't get close to each other. What is it? I love Trevor, and I want to be just as close to him as to the others, but I don't know how."

They knew the basic problems. That first year had been difficult when they cared for four children who were all under the age of five. Trevor was born as an "in-between" child since Tiffany was younger and a girl, and Troy had to work so hard to support Debbie during her recovery that he had little energy left for the "cuddling" that was such a natural part of fatherhood for him.

And on that fateful Thursday evening, one thought had haunted him like no other as he sat with Debbie, T.J., and Trent in the waiting area: *If only I could tell Trevor one more time how much he means to me! If only I could be sure he knew! Oh, God, don't let him die!*

Thank God, things turned out well Thursday night, but he *still* hadn't had the chance to talk with Trevor and tell him from the heart how much he loved him.

Troy enjoyed a very close relationship with his own father. In fact, as Troy reminisced about his father there in Trevor's room, Melvin Beam himself was recovering from a dangerous strain of flu in Carlisle

Regional Hospital. At the time of the accident, he already was fighting a losing battle with influenza in his home just up the hill from his son's home. In fact, that Saturday morning Melvin had talked with his son by phone from the hospital:

"Troy, when Debbie called us with the news that Trevor had been hurt on that harvester, I just broke down in tears. I was weak from fighting that flu bug, but when Anna [Troy's mother] told me he was being evacuated by Life Lion, I managed to make my way to the porch and watch them load him up.

"You know how we can see everything that goes on in the valley from up there on the hill. Well, I watched that helicopter lift off and fly right past us. Son, it just broke my heart. All I could say while I watched them fly away was, 'Poor little guy…Lord, protect him. Save his life and heal his body, in Jesus' name.'"

Suddenly the elevator doors opened and the sight of Dr. Boustred in surgical scrubs abruptly preempted every thought and memory that had occupied them through the previous 30-minute period. This was what they were waiting for.

"Well," Troy said, rising to greet the doctor, "How is he?"

The doctor looked at Troy and shook his head in wonder. "I've never seen anything like it," he replied. "Trevor's whole leg muscle has knitted together. There was no dead muscle or other tissue that we had to cut away. It's absolutely remarkable!"

Troy and Debbie felt their hearts soar. Troy looked across at Debbie and thought, *Is it possible for your smile to be any bigger?* Her face was radiant with joy. He could no longer contain it, so he said the first thing that came to mind: "Thank You, Lord!"

He had made his request known to the Lord. He and Debbie had prayed, asking for a miracle. And God had heard their cries.

Trevor came out from under sedation enough for Troy and Debbie to see him that evening just before they left for home that night. He nearly floored them with a totally unexpected announcement: "Mommy, my foot itches."

With a shocked expression, she and Troy quickly looked down at his right foot. It was totally wrapped up in an elastic bandage; only his toes were sticking out. Assuming that Trevor had no feeling in that right foot, she reached for his left foot.

"No," Trevor said, "my *right foot* is itching."

Debbie quickly glanced at Troy and reached out to touch the exposed toes of Trevor's right foot, but he immediately said, "No, Mama, further down."

She literally had to go all the way to Trevor's heel to find the itch. "What a *wonderful* itch!" she exclaimed, then looked at Troy as they laughed together with their son. It was obvious that God had healed Trevor's foot! Once again, it was clear that God was taking good care of Trevor.

Determined to grasp the scope and impossibility of what he was hearing, Troy recounted to himself the shopping list of impossibilities his little boy had faced.

This was the muscle that had been filleted open to the bone, much like the flesh of a fish is filleted or cut away from the bones.

This was part of the same leg muscle that had been hanging down around Trevor's ankle. (When a portion of it came loose and fell to the ground, Troy had to save it from his curious farm dogs!)

Now the doctor was saying *that same mutilated muscle* had knit together and begun to heal—*in just two days!*

From that time forward, the doctors *never* had to cut away any dead muscle tissue!

This was the turning point Troy and Debbie had prayed for. They knew then that God had meant what He had promised: "I'll take good care of him." Troy turned to Debbie excitedly and said:

"Debbie, I almost feel like the apostle Peter in prison: When the church prayed, *God moved.* [2] I've tried to imagine what it was like for Peter 2,000 years ago, but I didn't come close. Now we've *experienced the move of God for ourselves.* Can you feel the prayers of God's people being offered all around us?"

They had learned something else about Trevor's injuries the night before that had shocked them. Dr. Boustred told them something that is a part of Trevor's medical records to this day.

"Mr. and Mrs. Beam, when we finally conducted a complete examination of Trevor's injuries in the operating room, we found a puncture wound in his chest that alarmed us because it was positioned right over the heart. Evidently, one of the thick, pencil-sized prongs poked right through his chest wall.

"When we shined a light through the hole, we actually could see his lungs moving at the other end of the opening!

"That prong missed Trevor's heart by less than an inch! If it had been any closer, he would have died instantly."

It was obvious that God had worked yet another miracle for Trevor the day of the accident, giving him another chance. Troy felt he had personally received a second chance to redeem his relationship with a son "who was lost, but is now found."

Now it was his job to pray that God would heal this heart wound in the same way He was healing Trevor's physical wounds.

Endnotes

1. See Philippians 4:7.

2. See Acts 12:1-19.

CHAPTER FIVE

"GOD HEALED HIS FOOT"

Once Trevor's itch was taken care of, he finally drifted off into a deep sleep at 10 o'clock that night. Clearly, he was still feeling the effects of the sedation from the surgery.

Once they were sure Trevor was sleeping peacefully, Troy and Debbie kissed him gently and prepared to drive home. Before they left, Troy gave the nurse both their home phone number and his cell phone number and said, "If you have any questions, or if anything comes up—if you need me for *anything*—please don't hesitate to call me."

They drove home through the winter darkness and had barely settled into bed when the phone rang. When Troy flipped on the light, Debbie noticed the clock display: It was 12:45 a.m.

It was the nurse from the PICU at Penn State Hershey.

Now what? thought Troy as a chill shot through his body and his heart began to race like a runaway train. *It never fails. God gives you a peace that He is there, and then the devil tries to steal it away!*

"What is it?" Troy asked uneasily.

"Trevor is beside himself. He's all worked up. He keeps raising his head and tries to get up. I can't get him to lie still. I've tried giving him painkillers; I've tried everything I know to do to get him to go back to sleep, but all he says is that he wants his daddy. I'm afraid he's going to hurt himself."

Troy frowned, and Debbie could see that familiar look of determination settle over his countenance.

"Tell Trevor that Daddy is coming," Troy replied, trying to clear the fog from his brain so he could think critically about what lay before him. He knew the drive would take about an hour, so he added, "Ma'am, tell him that it will be a little while, but I'll be there."

As soon as he hung up, Troy quickly got dressed and drove back to the hospital. He arrived around 2:00 a.m., and just as he walked onto the PICU floor, the nurse came out of Trevor's room and saw him. She was shaking her head as she told him, "I can't believe it!"

"What can't you believe?"

"When I told Trevor, 'I've talked to your daddy and your daddy said he is coming; it may be a little while but he'll be here,' he lay back as though nothing had ever been wrong with him!"

As they approached Trevor's room, the nurse continued, "He just looked out of the window with such peace and tranquility," the nurse continued. "He has been lying there quietly, as content as could be, ever since!"

"What's so strange about that?" Troy asked.

"Mr. Beam," she answered, "I've worked with a lot of children facing serious situations on this floor. Now usually when I tell these children that their parents have said or promised something, it doesn't help. They continue to be restless and fearful."

Pausing just outside of Trevor's room, she added, "But when I told Trevor you said you were coming, it made all the difference with him."

What a blessing! Troy thought to himself. He was touched to realize that Trevor believed him when he had said he was coming. It seemed as though that was all the boy had needed to hear. *Perhaps my faith in my heavenly Father could be a little more like that,* he thought.

When Troy walked into Trevor's room, he was wide awake.

"Daddy, pull up a chair," he said, as if nothing had happened over the past three days. "I feel so much better when you're here with me."

Troy was amazed to see and hear his son doing so well after three long days in a near-comatose condition. He couldn't take his eyes off of Trevor's face as he pulled a chair close to the hospital bed and sat down in one of the few places where he could see his son in between the machines, wires, and tubes.

"Put your feet up here, Daddy," Trevor said with utmost sincerity, "and I'll rub them." Troy was stunned. This was his son, still confined to an intensive care hospital bed and only recently emerged from round-the-clock sedation, yet, here he was, offering to minister to his father.

Troy was touched beyond words. Part of him wanted to laugh at how well this boy knew his father, while the other part wanted to weep for the nearly dismembered child who was offering the only service he could in hopes that his daddy wouldn't leave him alone again.

"Son," Troy answered, "I'll stay right here with you, but if I put my feet up there for you to rub them, I may get so relaxed that I'll fall asleep. Then I might get my feet wrapped up in those cords and jerk something loose, and we can't have that. Listen, you can rub them later; I'd like that. But for now I'll just sit here with you. It's good just to hear your voice again now that the breathing tube is gone."

He wanted to make sure that Trevor knew he was there just for him because he loved him and not because he wanted a foot massage!

As they talked, Troy quickly realized once more that Trevor was still a little boy in a very serious crisis. It was clear that he was feeling a little fearful, so Troy looked at Trevor and said, "How about I just sit here and hold your hand?" Trevor looked up into his daddy's face with a great big smile and said, "Okay." They reached out and held each other's hand. Troy looked at Trevor and said, "I love you, Buddy."

Trevor drifted off to sleep in just a few minutes, a contented expression on his face.

Troy sat in the same position for a long time in those early morning hours before dawn, just holding his son's hand. It didn't matter to him that his neck was stiff and his backside had gone totally numb. He was literally *living out* the answer to the prayer he had prayed only a day ago. This was his second chance to connect with and communicate his deep love for Trevor.

When the hospital staff realized that Troy was trying to sleep in that little chair later that night, they quickly moved Trevor and his dad to a room that had a small cot. It wasn't much, but at least Troy could stretch out and lie down.

Debbie arrived with some of the children that Sunday morning by 10 o'clock—once she had organized the household and checked on the children who remained behind.

Troy was still nursing a stiff neck when another doctor entered the room that afternoon to greet the family.

He glanced at Trevor, saw that he was asleep, and announced with a broad smile, "Well, I have good news. It looks like we will be able to save Trevor's right leg after all."

Of course, Troy and Debbie already knew this from their earlier visits. They also knew something that none of the doctors or nurses knew yet: *Trevor had feeling in his severely damaged right foot.*

The medical team had said Trevor probably wouldn't have any feeling in his foot because the primary nerve was damaged. This nerve damage was important because if Trevor didn't have feeling in his foot, he would have trouble simply moving it, let alone walking or running on it.

Troy smiled as he thought back to the "itching announcement" the previous night and Debbie's expedition to scratch that "wonderful itch." Then he had to wrestle his mind back to the moment because the doctor was still talking to them in earnest tones.

"Look, Mr. and Mrs. Beam, we *will* be able to save Trevor's right leg, but your boy probably won't have any feeling or movement in his foot because the muscle and its adjoining nerves have been torn so badly."

Troy and Debbie glanced at one another, fighting to hold back smiles because of their shared secret. The doctor was a dedicated physician, and he must have been puzzled because these parents just weren't reacting to his warnings about the limitations of modern medicine the way he expected them to.

They continued to listen patiently as the doctor covered in detail each problem Trevor could face because of his extensive injuries. The problem was that they already knew that their son had been healed.

Finally Troy found a spot in the conversation where he could politely break in.

"We hear what you are saying, doctor, but Trevor already has moved his foot and has feeling in it."

It was as if he hadn't spoken a word. The doctor continued to explain his lengthy litany of the potential complications, possible problems, and probable challenges Trevor would face.

Troy glanced at Debbie and shook his head while wondering, *Didn't he hear me? Is he ignoring me?*

Finally, he looked the doctor in the eye and said, "Doctor, Trevor has feeling and movement in his foot."

A puzzled look suddenly spread across the doctor's face. After a brief pause, he asked, "Are you sure *you* didn't move it?"

"Yes, I am. I did not move his foot."

Just as this conversation was winding down, Trevor woke up. So Debbie decided in her direct way to weigh in on the discussion. She uncovered Trevor's foot and nodded to Troy, who said, "Trevor, wiggle your toes for me."

Although he couldn't move his foot very well because of the bandages, he did manage to wiggle his toes. Debbie's smile lit the room as Troy started to rub Trevor's foot and said, "Can you feel Daddy touching your foot?"

"Yes," Trevor replied.

The doctor may have assumed that Trevor's answer was merely a positive reply to a positive question, or his scientific training simply may have required him to check for himself under more rigorous standards.

Whatever the reason, he walked to the other side of Trevor's bed, pulled out his ink pen, and held it a half-inch away from Trevor's foot. Since Trevor was lying down, he couldn't see what the doctor was doing. "Trevor," he said, "can you feel me touching your foot?"

After a few seconds, Trevor said, "No." He sounded disappointed because he assumed the doctor *was* touching his foot, but Trevor was right. The doctor wasn't touching his foot.

Determined to eliminate any chance for misleading responses, the doctor touched Trevor's little toe without a word or an obvious movement that he could see. Then the doctor asked again, "Can you feel me touching your foot now?"

"Yes," Trevor answered.

"Where?"

"My little toe."

The doctor then moved the pen to Trevor's big toe, again without a word or obvious movement. "Trevor, can you feel me touching your foot?"

"Yes."

"Where?"

"My big toe."

Perhaps determined to eliminate the possibility that Trevor was just a good guesser, the doctor moved his pen away with a slight unobservable movement and then asked once more in the same tone of voice he had used in each previous question: "Trevor, can you feel me touching your foot?"

"No," Trevor answered. Once again he was right.

As a trained scientific skeptic, the doctor tried to confuse Trevor by touching the pen between his toes.

"Trevor, can you feel me touching your foot now?"

"Yes."

"Where?"

"Between my toes."

Finally, the doctor put his pen back in his pocket, shook his head, and walked away from the bedside. What could he say? The clear evidence of a miracle could not be denied.

The Beams never again heard him say that their son would have no feeling or movement in his foot.

By this time, Troy and Debbie felt as if they were floating among the clouds. They had gone from the valley to the mountaintop in only three days. They still didn't know what the ultimate outcome would be, but they knew that God had divinely touched Trevor's leg and foot. They had dared to ask God for a miracle—and He had delivered!

Long after the doctor had left, the excitement just kept growing in the Trevor Beam hospital room. Even the children joined in the joyful reliving of the miracles that day. Trevor especially enjoyed the way he never seemed to run out of volunteers to scratch that pesky itch!

Finally, Trevor's "batteries" ran down, and he fell asleep for the night. Debbie knew she needed to get the children home, even though she wasn't looking forward to driving home without Troy.

With this major battle won, it was time for a new strategy in the Beam household. Troy and Debbie had already talked about it.

Trevor wouldn't be sedated as much from this point on, and he really wanted one of his parents to be with him every day—and they agreed it was necessary. That meant they would have to continue in "split shifts" to run their family, the farm, and the businesses *and* be there for Trevor.

Despite his fatigue and stiff neck from spending the previous night in a chair, Troy volunteered for the first solo shift. Debbie would take the children home in the van. It wouldn't be easy, but there was no other way.

While Debbie and the children made their way home, Troy settled in for another night in Trevor's room, but his mind continually examined and reexamined the flurry of events, emotions, and unexplainable things that had happened in their lives during the previous 36 hours.

I'd have loved to see God give us an outright miracle by instantaneously healing Trevor's leg, he thought to himself. *But God chose to work differently. I know He can and does work instant miracles like that. After all, He created our bodies. He can heal them completely and totally with no signs or evidence that anything was ever wrong.*

Troy looked out the window of that hospital room for a glimmer of stars or the moon in the winter night and suddenly sensed the familiar presence of the Lord right there with him. Then he grinned before praying out loud as he gazed up into the heavens:

"Most of the time, Lord, it seems like You choose the slower path of healing—one miracle at a time. It sure seems to take a lot more faith that way—at least from my puny perspective here on earth. And since that's the way You've chosen to heal Trevor, that's fine.

"We're just so grateful that You have brought these healing miracles to our son! I promised You, 'Lord, in Your time, in Your way, to Your glory.' You know I meant it then and that I mean it now.

"You know how long You want us to stay at the medical center. You also know how many people You want us to talk to and how many lives You want to touch. Thank You, Lord, for being in control. Help Debbie and I to learn how to rest in You."

CHAPTER SIX

"YOU'VE ENCOURAGED ME..."

Troy and Debbie split their time at the hospital to keep life stable in their home and to maintain the businesses. Troy stayed with Trevor Thursdays through Mondays so Debbie could nurture and care for the children at home. Debbie took her post on Tuesdays and Wednesdays so that Troy could catch up with his work on the farm and manage the construction business and properties.

The miracles of divine intervention that saved Trevor's life and then saved his right leg and foot deeply encouraged them and reassured them that God was still in "the healing business" today—no matter what men, institutions, or so-called experts might say to the contrary.

It was ironic that the miracles took place within the walls of one of the nation's most respected pediatric trauma centers, where the facts of Trevor's case systematically were documented and fully verified.

Yet, even with the incredible string of miracles they had seen, Troy and Debbie knew they would face even more challenges in the days ahead. They relied on the peace of God to carry them through day by day.

With each new day, the Beams experienced new opportunities to see how Trevor's accident and ongoing miraculous recovery impacted the lives of other people.

In fact, they quickly noticed that from the moment Trevor's leg began to heal miraculously only two days after his catastrophic accident, it became almost impossible to sleep in the hospital. Hospitals generally aren't considered great "hotels" anyway, but night and day a steady stream of doctors and nurses walked into Trevor's room to see him and marvel over the healing that was taking place.

People who simply visit friends or relatives in a hospital or perhaps spend a short time under treatment themselves may not understand this, but hospitals can be very depressing places to work.

Many doctors and nurses—especially those dealing with serious trauma cases or long-term debilitating diseases such as cancer or other virtually impossible cases—often deliver bad news to parents and family members several times each day. Although the patients and family members bear the brunt of the pain in these cases, those who care for them pay a dear price as well.

At times, even the most dedicated medical care providers may find themselves going through their rounds like robots. It is for this reason that so many of them seem to separate themselves from emotional involvement with their patients—they often detach themselves from the pain around them simply for their own emotional survival.

That is why anything approaching a miracle or a medical wonder attracts so much attention. It revives hope in people dedicated to helping people get well. Even one miraculous turnaround can spark a wildfire of hope and renewed vision in a hospital or medical center.

The Beam family soon realized that every time a shift changed, they could expect anywhere from six to a dozen or more hospital staffers to walk in and line both sides of Trevor's bed! One day when Debbie was there, a nurse came in to make an interesting observation.

"In my 20 years of nursing, I have never seen anyone receive the kind of company Trevor is getting. Now, I'm not talking about the regular friends and family who come to visit with your son. We're used to that; it helps our patients heal quicker. No, I'm talking about all of the hospital staff—especially all of the doctors and nurses—who came into this room to see Trevor."

"Why is that?" Debbie asked curiously. When Debbie relayed the nurse's answer to Troy, it once again reminded him of the late-night prayer he made to the Lord on the highway between the hospital and their farm.

"They all have heard about the extent and the trauma of Trevor's injuries when he was admitted. When we tell them how well he is doing, they just can't believe it. So they have to come to see it for themselves. They can't believe that Trevor has feeling and movement in his foot."

To this day, Trevor has a stronger pulse in his right foot than in his left.

It was Troy's turn to talk with a nurse the day she came in to give Trevor some pain medication. For the first few days of Trevor's hospital stay, the trauma team had administered an epidural (a spinal pain block commonly used to numb all pain sensation from the waist down for childbirth and other situations involving intense pain).

After that, the doctors switched to morphine and strong doses of Tylenol with codeine on a regular basis, assuming he needed the medication to control pain while his serious injuries healed.

Oddly enough, Trevor often told his parents that the medicine made him sick. It seemed that almost every form of pain medicine they gave him made him nauseous. However, he *never* complained of any pain throughout the ordeal.

On this particular day, Trevor said, "Daddy, can I skip the medicine this time?"

Troy looked across at his son with a surprised expression, but simply said, "It's up to you, son. If you want to try to get through the bandage changes and everything else without the pain medicine, I don't mind if you don't take it."

He had watched the nurses change the extensive bandages that nearly covered Trevor's body. He knew grown men had been driven to tears during bandage changes for such extensive injuries.

"I don't want it anymore," Trevor said with a look of determination.

So when the nurse walked in with his daily prescription of pain medicine, Troy said, "He doesn't want that anymore."

She looked at Trevor and then at Troy in surprise and asked, "Are you sure?"

"I'm not preventing you from using it," Troy reassured her. "Now if Trevor wants it and if he says he is hurting, then you certainly have my permission to give it to him. But he doesn't want it. It makes him vomit. He wants to try going without it."

"All right, if the doctor says it's okay," the nurse said with some reluctance.

So Trevor stopped taking his pain medication. The news seemed to spread quickly enough that everyone started wondering how he would react when it was time to change his bandages.

Everyone at the nurses' station seemed to be both shocked and relieved when Trevor calmly responded to every request his nurses made as they changed his numerous bandages.

"Trevor, does this hurt? No?"

"Now roll slightly to the right—this probably *will* hurt, but we'll be as gentle as we can."

In fact, Troy noticed that the only people "grimacing" in pain were the nurses, who had grown used to empathizing with the pain their patients usually experienced during such extensive bandage changes. They clearly were surprised and pleased when Trevor actually responded to the procedure even more calmly than when he was given the medication!

It didn't take long for the news to spread.

The head nurse on the next shift walked into Trevor's room and bluntly asked Troy, "What are you doing for pain control? I review Trevor's medication orders each day, and I noticed there is no prescription here for any pain medicine."

Troy didn't answer immediately, and during the short pause she added, "What are you doing for pain control? Do you pray, or what?"

"Yes, we pray." he replied. "There are a lot of prayers being said on his behalf."

The instant the nurse asked the question about prayer for Trevor, his mind involuntarily flashed back to the time that Will stopped by to ask about Trevor. Will often provided masonry work for Troy as a subcontractor.

He mentioned that he had heard Trevor was in an accident, so Troy began to tell him about all of the miraculous things God had done since the accident. When he began to describe his encounter with God in the shower, of all places, Troy noticed the shocked look on his friend's face. Will swallowed hard and in a very serious voice said, "What time were you in the shower?"

"I don't know, Will. I'm not really in the habit of documenting my shower time," Troy replied with a grin. "Why?"

Will's answer caught him totally off guard.

"Troy, I've never had anything like this happen to me before. I was in the shower on Saturday night too, and *God spoke to me!* He told me to kneel down and pray for Trevor."

What an awesome God! Troy thought to himself. Just one week before Trevor's accident, the two of them had been discussing business. Troy briefly mentioned some challenges he was facing at the time.

"Are you serious? Aren't you worried about the situation?" Will had asked. "I think I'd line up a whole battery of lawyers and fight to win with a show of force."

"No, I'm just not worried about it."

"That's exactly what I'm saying, Troy. I can't understand why you aren't worried right now," Will said. "How can you act so peaceful when anyone else would want to start World War III over it?"

"You can have peace all the time," Troy said, "when your peace comes from Jesus Christ. Have you ever heard about the plan of salvation?"

"What's that?"

Troy quickly thought about how to explain it, then said,

"Will, it's really simple. God doesn't want *anyone* to be lost. He offers salvation to every one of us, but He leaves the choice in our hands.

"Jesus said in John 3:16: *'For God so loved the world, that he gave his only begotten Son, that whosoever believeth in him should not perish, but have everlasting life.'*

"Will, it's as simple as believing. None of us is good enough to earn salvation—only Jesus was good enough, so He paid the price for our sin by giving up His life for you and me.

"The Bible says in Romans 10:9 that if you confess with your mouth the Lord Jesus and believe in your heart that God raised Him from the dead, then you will be saved. That's all it takes, Will. Just believe."

Just one week later, Will was in the shower when he sensed God telling him to pray for Trevor. Will told Troy, "I told the Lord, 'I don't know how to pray. I've never prayed before.' And He said, 'Just get down and pray.' So I got down on my knees and prayed."

When Troy called Will on the phone and told him how Trevor's leg and foot had been healed, he said, "This is just too spooky for me, Troy." As they talked about how real God is, Will couldn't get over how God actually asked him to pray so specifically for Trevor.

Troy shook his head as he remembered Will's amazement over the miracle that followed his prayer, then looked up when Trevor said, "Dad, my foot." He knew what that meant. Whenever Trevor mentioned his foot (it usually was itchy, probably as a part of the healing process), it was a signal for Troy or Debbie to rub his foot. Troy thought, *Trevor, don't complain now; I just told the nurse we prayed!*

As Troy walked to the bed to help his son, the nurse who had asked if he prayed for Trevor said, "I'll...I'll wait outside for a few minutes that way you can do your thing." Then she quickly stepped outside the room and carefully closed the door.

Shaking his head with a wry grin, Troy rubbed Trevor's foot and then helped him into his wheelchair for their daily game of air hockey in the game room. As they left Trevor's room, the nurse looked up with a smile and said, "I guess it works!"

Trevor craned his neck around to look at his father, shielded his mouth with his hand, and whispered, "What did she think you were doing?"

"I don't know," replied Troy, shaking his head. "Maybe some sort of rain dance."

Whatever was going through the minds of the professionals on staff, they seemed to have one thing in common: They were in awe of what had happened to Trevor and of his rapid recovery.

It became more and more obvious to Troy and Debbie with each passing day that God was using Trevor's situation to reveal His power and love to everyone who came into contact with him.

After Trevor had beaten Troy at air hockey once more, they returned to the room. As if on cue, the head nurse reappeared in the doorway. "Excuse me, guys. Do you mind if I bring in my crew?"

Troy looked at Trevor and shrugged. When Trevor nodded his permission, he said, "I suppose not. What do they want?"

"Well," she answered, "everyone's heard about Trevor. They all want to come in and meet him and hear your story."

By this time the "story" was getting longer every day, not because anyone was exaggerating, but because God was doing so much all at once. It was as if the miracles were accelerating over time!

Whenever Troy or Debbie described all of the things that had happened, there was something new to add each time. Someone would come forward with new information, a new development, or some fresh element of God's love, mercy, and healing power in Trevor's ongoing healing.

On this particular night, Troy invited all of them into the room, wondering in the back of his mind, *What will these nurses make of Trevor's story?*

He pulled out a picture he carried displaying the harvester wagon in which Trevor had been injured and began to describe in straightforward fashion everything he could remember about the accident.

He even described the morning he had prayed shortly after the accident and the time he had prayed in the shower—and the whole time they stood listening silently. It seemed as if they couldn't stop gazing at the picture of the silage wagon—and at Trevor smiling at them from his bed. No one could figure out how anyone could live after being pulled through the beater bars shown in the picture.

After that impromptu meeting in Trevor's packed hospital room, the various staff members would ask about Trevor and his progress every time Troy saw one of them in the hallway or cafeteria. It seemed that everyone who knew about Trevor always wanted to know more.

One of the hospital counselors once asked, "Troy, you tell that story to everybody, don't you?"

"It's worth telling," he replied in his typically brief fashion. Trevor wasn't walking yet, but everyone knew he had received a divine touch.

During those stressful early days after the accident, a representative from the hospital administration approached Troy and said, "Mr. Beam, we are aware of your son's traumatic accident, as well as of the serious aftereffects that nearly always challenge family members who are close. Would you like to speak with a counselor about your situation?"

Troy thought, *I am already at peace with God in this situation; what could anyone say that would help more than that?* At first he politely refused, not wanting to offend someone making such a kind and compassionate offer. However, when a representative asked again, he accepted. He was curious to learn what kind of counsel a trained secular counselor would give to a father in his position.

A short time later, when Trevor went into surgery to have his bandage changed (this was routine in the first few days after the accident), a counselor came into the hospital room to talk with Troy.

As they shook hands, Troy thought to himself, *I don't think I'm going to say much; I want to see what kind of advice I'll be given.*

Pete had served as a counselor at Penn State Hershey for several years. When he was first assigned the Beam case, he took a deep breath and just sat at his desk looking at the file. *This one won't be easy,* he mused. Because the hospital's Pediatric Intensive Care Unit had won fame for its expertise in difficult trauma cases with children, many of the worst cases in the region were routed through its doors. To put it plainly, he was used to working with families facing impossible and painful circumstances. This one was right at the top of the list.

The moment he saw Troy, with his square jaw, broad shoulders, and work-calloused hands, he knew he was dealing with a strong man. His first glance into Troy's eyes confirmed to him that this man was as tough and resilient inside as he appeared to be on the outside.

After their introduction, Pete began by mentioning to Troy that people who experience tragedy such as the Beams had experienced often suffer from nightmares, intense guilt, fear, and intense remorse over seemingly endless "what-if-I..." scenarios. One of the most serious trends is that other children in the family can be affected seriously by these things.

After warning Troy that the aftereffects of tragedies like this have broken up homes, Pete offered some practical advice on how to talk with the children and how to help Trevor recover emotionally as well as physically.

Troy didn't make it easy for Pete. He always had a tendency to listen more than he talked, and he usually reserved any opinions or feedback until he heard out what a person had to say. On this day, he was reserved even more because he had set his course to listen exclusively.

Pete delivered his standard speech, but he was puzzled when he didn't get much feedback—positive or negative. Troy simply sat and listened, only nodding his head occasionally and giving monosyllabic responses.

Troy didn't intend to irritate Pete, but it was obvious that the counselor was growing frustrated. Finally, Pete said, "Well, tell me what happened!"

Troy laid out the whole story from the beginning: the accident, the prayers, the healings, the sense of peace... everything. It was the counselor's turn to listen. Troy even told him how they had prayed that morning and how God was blessing his family and had been so good to them.

He was still talking with Pete when one of the nurses came in to say that Trevor was coming out of the operating room. Troy immediately stood up and excused himself.

"Sorry, Pete, but I really need to go to the recovery room. Trevor always wants me to be there with him in the recovery room because he gets nauseous every time he regains consciousness from anesthesia.

He won't throw up if I'm there to hold his hand, rub his forehead, and speak softly to him. I don't know why it works; perhaps just knowing that his daddy is with him helps Trevor relax."

Pete stood up to walk out of the room with Troy, and as they walked down the hallway he said, "Troy, you've encouraged me more than I could ever encourage you! Do you think we could talk again sometime?" Pete hesitated for a moment. Then in all sincerity he said, "I want to hear how you got your experience with Jesus."

"I suppose so," Troy replied. And with a wry smile he added, "I'll probably be here for awhile."

Thank You, Lord, he prayed silently as he walked down the hall. *I guess we really are at this medical center for a larger reason than simply to get medical care for my injured son. You weren't the cause or source of this tragic accident, but You have placed us here — and that includes Trevor and Debbie, too — for a deeper and greater purpose.*

Over the next few days, the counselor was true to his word. He did return to Trevor's room to talk with Troy and Trevor. He heard numerous stories from Troy's life. He learned what Troy had seen God do in his family, how he had met his wife, welcomed the birth of his seven children, and how he met his Savior. In fact, from that time forward to the last day of Trevor's hospital stay, Pete came to talk with Troy every day.

CHAPTER SEVEN

"YOU DON'T KNOW MY DADDY"

Troy and Debbie became fixtures at the medical center as one week after another went by. Trevor, meanwhile, became Penn State Hershey's unintended VIP guest and most-visited patient.

A steady stream of nurses, doctors, and medical students continued to flow through Trevor's room. Debbie still smiles when she remembers how the lights constantly flipped on by the hour—1:00 a.m.—2:00 a.m.—3:00 a.m.—4:00 a.m.

The most common question of the entire stay became, "Trevor, can you wiggle your toes for us?" Debbie confided to Troy, "I wonder if Trevor will ever get a full night of rest until we get home?"

Since Trevor's most serious injury (and most significant miracle) involved his nearly amputated right leg and right foot, the preferred place to take his pulse inevitably was his right foot. Ever the mother, Debbie worried about the "blue goo" the medical staff used to lubricate Trevor's foot each time they checked his pulse with a Doppler ultrasound unit.

One time a doctor conducting the Doppler test for a group of medical students noticed Debbie staring at the blue goo. He reassured her, "I know it looks nasty, but Trevor won't have a blue foot forever. It *does* wash off… *eventually.*" She smiled and said matter-of-factly, "I'm relieved to hear it," as the students chuckled politely.

The procedure of checking Trevor's pulse in his right foot with the Doppler unit seemed to be a favorite pastime among the students there, so it was a good thing the Beams found it humorous. Troy summed up their attitude with the casual comment to Debbie, "I guess everyone is happy to see how well Trevor is coming along."

Trevor's nurses faithfully checked his vital signs around the clock, and they diligently monitored his progress, checked his bandages and the wounds under them, and dispensed any necessary medications.

However, since Troy and Debbie stayed with Trevor around the clock, they gradually took over more and more of his daily care routines. The nurses were glad to see parents take such a personal, hands-on interest in their hospitalized child; it was something they wished would happen far more often.

Ill and injured children always seemed to mend more quickly and with fewer complications when parents stayed on-site and remained personally involved in their child's recovery.

So the nursing staff was more than happy to allow the Beams to help with the day-to-day tasks of bathing, the use of the bedpan, and other functions that Trevor could not yet do for himself. (He quickly had discovered how many things were difficult to handle alone when wrapped like a mummy with one foot kept elevated and immobile.)

Whenever they could arrange it, Troy and Debbie also brought along one or two of their other children to spend time with Trevor. They had an unswerving goal to keep their family connected and close through this ordeal.

His face lit up every time a brother or sister entered his room, and he seemed to forget that he was in a hospital as long as a sibling was there.

T.J. and Trent were nearly as helpful as Troy and Debbie at the hospital—extending their roles as the "oldest boys and sub-supervisors" from the farm to Trevor's room. It seemed to help them avoid the "guilt trap" that Troy was so determined that they avoid. As a result, their good times with Trevor in Hershey helped them continue their vital work maintaining much of the farm routine back home.

Tiffany was younger, but she took to the "nursing" role naturally and almost took over "Jakey's" care (that was her pet name for Trevor) whenever she was "on duty" in his room. Despite the obvious evidence that Trevor was recovering from extremely serious injuries, the twins talked and carried on as if nothing had happened and no time had been lost.

As far as they were concerned, everything would be fine as long as they could be together. This, as much as anything, helped restore a feeling of "normal" to Trevor's life during the difficult weeks he spent in the hospital. Virtually every nurse, doctor, or orderly who stepped into the room when Tiffany and Trevor were talking had to interrupt their own routine just to stare and marvel at the two blond-haired twins laughing and talking as if no one else was in the room.

Although Travis and Tiara, the two youngest in the Beam family at two years and one year of age respectively, had to stay home with "Ma and Pappy" through most of Trevor's hospital stay, four-year-old Tyler more than made up for the infrequent visits with his endless questions, boundless energy, and joyful spirit.

Taken together, the siblings played games with Trevor, ran to get him drinks of water or snacks, scratched his endless itches, rubbed his feet, and were just "there" for him in ways that only brothers or sisters can. The younger ones especially were awed by the hospital cafeteria and the fact that Trevor could order anything on the menu anytime he wanted to eat. They couldn't believe their brother could order his favorites—French fries or pizza—at the touch of a button!

It was Tyler, the "4-year-old going on 14," who supplied some of the most interesting highlights for Troy and Debbie during his visits to Trevor.

One time Troy and Debbie brought Tyler along for a weekend stay at the hospital. While they were driving from the farm to Hershey, Tyler asked in typical four-year-old straightforward fashion, "What if Trevor had died in the wagon, Daddy? Would he be in heaven right now?"

Without any hesitation, Troy said, "Yes, he would be there right now."

Tyler thought about the answer for a moment before replying in a sober tone, "I wouldn't want to die."

Troy glanced at his son to gauge his reaction and smiled before he continued.

"Tyler, he would be up there having so much fun that he wouldn't want to come back! You wouldn't either, if you knew what is up there. It's so wonderful and grand up there, you'd feel sorry for us down here. And you couldn't wait until we could be there, too."

Little Tyler's eyes widened with wonder. Troy could almost see his imagination take off. "What's up there?" he asked, almost breathless with wonder.

"Well, it's so good that God is keeping it a secret. He won't tell us yet because He's saving it for a big, big surprise!"

Tyler thought on his daddy's words for several minutes as the sounds of the tires humming on the pavement and the whistling of the wind took over the truck cab. But finally he looked up at Troy and then over at Debbie before he boldly announced, "I want to die, Mommy; why can't I die? I want to go to heaven and have fun."

Debbie shot a quick glance at Troy before she reached out to draw Tyler close in a warm hug. She said, "Well, Tyler, there are people down here who don't know that they can go to heaven. Since you know about it, God may want you to stay here for quite awhile and tell people what you know. Then they can believe it and go, too."

With a look of resignation that made Tyler look far older than his tender four years, he said, "I guess so. But I *still* want to die!"

From Trevor's first week in the hospital, he had received lots of gifts from people wanting to wish him well and help encourage him in the recovery process. One donor, in particular, demonstrated some remarkable creativity by sending Trevor an entire month's worth of gifts, featuring one gift to be opened each day.

None of Trevor's brothers or sisters ever seemed to feel bad or "left out" by all the attention Trevor received. However, Tyler showed yet another side to his emerging personality when he told his daddy one day, "I want to get hurt so I can get all those gifts!" When Troy quickly glanced at him, he noticed that familiar mischievous twinkle in Tyler's eye. He just shook his head and grinned over his son's dry sense of humor.

The long and crooked five-inch gash on the top of Trevor's head had closed and the stitches had been removed by that time. The doctors also had removed the drainage tube they had placed through the hole in Trevor's chest that was roughly the size of a half-dollar coin to help it drain and heal.

Each time another tube or cable was removed, it seemed that Trevor's movements and energy level would visibly increase. So did his curiosity.

Although his left femur was snapped in half in the accident, doctors had delayed putting a cast on the leg because it was a "compound fracture" in which the broken bone had pierced the skin, increasing the risk for infection. (As bad as it was, it was actually called Trevor's "good leg".) They had to pin it together using a plate and screws, then simply wrapped it tightly in bandages.

Later on, when Trevor had a chance to see how his leg had healed, he asked, "Why did they cut me so crooked on my left leg?" Troy replied, "Honey, they didn't! That's where your bone came out when it broke!"

One morning about three weeks after Trevor's accident, Troy decided to propose a radical change in Trevor's recovery plan when the doctor checked in to evaluate Trevor's progress.

"You know, doctor, I think we can take care of Trevor better at home than we can here. That way I could help care for him and still get my work done. And it would be less disruptive for our other children.

"Can he go home? I could bring him back in for checkups any time you felt he needed it."

The doctor looked up from the thick stack of medical charts on Trevor that he was studying and nodded.

"Yes, I heard you were taking care of him. According to the nurses on this floor, you and your wife are working them out of a job here!

"Before we can release him, however, there is some paperwork we need to take care of. We don't want to leave any detail uncovered or left undone that might set back Trevor's progress. We have to make sure everything is done correctly and in order, but I promise you we'll let you know just as soon as Trevor can go home."

Trevor didn't even try to suppress the smile on his face upon hearing the good news. Debbie was on the schedule to take over for Troy the next day, so it was Debbie who was "on duty" on Tuesday, the day Trevor's doctor alerted them that he could leave the hospital and go home the following morning.

Debbie didn't know whether to laugh or cry as she dialed Troy's number, so she did a little of both as she told Troy the good news. All of the Beam children had been waiting anxiously for a call ever since Troy and Debbie told them Trevor would be coming home soon.

So as soon as the phone rang that night, Troy had six sets of ears crowding closer as he answered the phone. "Now get back, now; give me some room to answer the phone, kids," he said as he recognized Debbie's voice. "It's Mom. Let's see what news she has for us."

"Troy, the doctor says Trevor can come home *tomorrow — tomorrow morning!*"

"Praise God!" Troy exclaimed, with tears beginning to well up in his eyes. "That's the news I've been waiting to hear for weeks! Did you hear that, everybody? Trevor's coming home!

"Honey, I'll be there in the morning with the van to bring both of you back home. Hand the phone to Trevor, will you?"

"Hi, Daddy."

"Hi there, Buddy. I hear you're coming home! Are you sure you can bear to leave all of that good food and special attention from all of those nice nurses?"

"Come on, Daddy! You *know* I can't wait to get back home and be with everybody. Does everybody know yet?"

"Yeah, they all know. In fact, they're all here crowding me so much that I can hardly move!"

Then Troy had the children pass the phone from one to the other to talk with Trevor. The older ones helped the younger kids manage the phone without dropping it.

As the children talked, Troy quietly stepped outside to check the weather. He'd had an uneasy feeling all day as he worked at the farm and checked on his various construction projects in the area.

For most of his life, he had done outside work, and he had worked through some of the most severe weather Pennsylvania had seen—and that is saying a lot. All day long he had sensed that a major winter storm was about to hit the area.

Suddenly Troy spun on his heel and walked back into the house with his mind mentally checking off a list of emergency preparations for the storm—one list was for the family, the house, and the farm. Everybody who lived in that mostly rural area knew the drill: firewood, flashlights, food and water reserves, heating oil, backup generators, cell phones charged to the maximum level, and full fuel tanks in all vehicles and reserve tanks.

The second list was for the trip he would make tomorrow—no matter what happened with the weather. And it began with a plan and a backup plan to get him from home to hospital and back in one piece.

In their most recent "hospital duty" cycle, Troy and Debbie had used the same vehicle to shuttle between the farm and the hospital. Troy had come home planning to return over the weekend and allow Debbie to drive back and leave him at the hospital if necessary. Now he liked the new plan much better—much, *much* better.

It took awhile for Troy to get the kids settled into bed that night, and he understood why. He was as excited as they were. As a soft silence settled over the Beam home disturbed only by the sounds of cattle lowing and an occasional bark from the dogs, Troy thought of his wife and son in Hershey. *Finally, we can bring Trevor home. Thank You, Lord!*

Debbie and Trevor were slow to get to bed as well. The hospital room and long halls of the pediatric wing had been Trevor's home-away-from-home for three weeks, but he couldn't wait to get back home to the farm. His mind was filled with thoughts about his reunion with his brothers and sisters, how the dogs were doing, and which of the cows had given birth while he was gone.

He couldn't wait to settle into his favorite place on the couch in the living room, wiggle under his favorite comforter, and talk to Tiffany, his twin sister and best friend.

Trevor was still imagining his first day back home when he drifted off to sleep, with the sound of his mother's voice in the background as she softly read Psalm 91 from the Bible.

Troy opened his eyes in the total darkness of his bedroom a good hour before the sun rose that Wednesday morning. He immediately knew his suspicions about the weather had been correct. He could hear the wind blowing and the telltale sounds of the dangerous mix of sleet and driven snow hitting the windows and the tin roof of the farmhouse.

A *major* winter storm had hit, and he knew without even checking that the roads were covered with ice.

He wasn't too concerned about the weather, however. Like so many locals whose lives had been spent in year-round livestock and construction operations in the region, he was used to the rugged weather that could descend on the area.

Winter storms and deep snowfalls were common in south central Pennsylvania, and he would take them in stride. All he could see in his mind were the happy faces of his son and wife waiting for him to come and take them home.

It wasn't until he started driving on the highway toward the hospital that Troy realized just how bad the weather was. He quickly discovered that a tractor-trailer rig had rolled over on the Interstate, and later he learned that the emergency rooms at medical centers along the route were jammed.

Meanwhile, Debbie was waiting with Trevor at the hospital unaware of the intensity of the winter storm swirling outside the hospital room windows. As they talked together about what Trevor wanted to see and do when he got home, a nurse came into the room.

"Trevor, I'm afraid you probably won't get to go home today. The roads are bad; there's a lot of ice out there. Your daddy probably won't be able to make it."

For a split second Trevor's eyes looked sober. But only for a second. Then shaking his head, Trevor gave her a big smile. He looked up at his mother and smiled again. The nurse was puzzled. This just wasn't the reaction she had expected.

She looked at Debbie and Trevor and quickly realized she was about to be included in a secret that mother and son shared with obvious joy. Debbie smiled and looked at Trevor while gently squeezing his hand, and the eight-year-old aimed his disarming blue eyes and winning smile at the unsuspecting nurse before he confidently said, "You don't know my daddy!"

Trevor was a young man who believed what his father said. The night Troy promised that he would be at the hospital, he had arrived right when he said he would despite the early morning hour.

"I'm sure you're right, Trevor. Your daddy is a very remarkable man," the nurse said as she left the room. But secretly, she thought, *I hope that precious young man won't be disappointed. He was so excited about going home.*

She quickly forgot about the exchange as her thoughts switched to her shift change later that morning. She wasn't prepared to spend the day and night at work, stranded by a storm nobody wanted and few were prepared for.

Trevor was *still* thinking about the conversation, however. *If Daddy said he would be here this morning to take me and Mommy home, then it will happen. Daddy always keeps his word.*

That was all he needed. In his mind, he returned to daydreaming about what he would be doing in his own room in a few hours. His daddy was coming! It didn't matter to Trevor what anyone might say about his daddy's chances of beating the storm; they just didn't know his daddy.

Troy Beam walked onto Trevor's floor at the medical center by 10:00 a.m. that morning, still brushing off the snow that had quickly accumulated on his coat during his brisk walk from the parking lot to the hospital building.

When the nurse looked up and recognized Troy, she fell in step behind him. *I owe Trevor the chance to tell me 'I told you so,'* she mused to herself. As they walked into Trevor's hospital room, his eyes lit up and then he leaned to one side to catch her glance. "See, I told you he would come. Now *that's* my daddy!"

"You sure were right, Trevor!" she said. "And I'm glad for you. Now you be sure to tell your brothers and sisters hello for all of us on the floor, will you?" Then she left to gather the discharge papers the Beams would have to sign before Trevor left the hospital.

When Troy and Debbie were ready to take Trevor home, Troy went to tell the doctors they were leaving and to thank them for their care for Trevor. He was pleased to see that Bill, a counselor who had noticed Troy telling Trevor's story to the hospital staff weeks earlier, was standing in his office door further down the hallway.

"Troy, I really don't know what to say to you," he said, raising his voice slightly to cover the distance between them. "You are already an encouragement. You've encouraged all of us."

"Well," Troy replied, "the only thing I can say is that this has been one blessed experience."

When Troy had replied to Bill, he saw Paul, the counselor assigned to the Beam's case, standing further down the hall, listening. Troy sensed that he needed to take an extra effort to say his good-byes to

Paul. *I know Debbie and Trevor are waiting, he thought to himself rapidly, but the paperwork pile is still waiting for another inch or two of forms and duplicate forms before Trevor can finally go through the front exit.*

He had already had the opportunity to tell the counselor about Trevor's accident and God's miraculous healing and delivering power, and he had shared his personal experience of receiving Jesus Christ as Savior.

Suddenly, Troy motioned to Debbie, and after she nodded, he walked over to Paul to say good-bye.

"You're taking Trevor home already?" Paul asked. "Well, I'll walk with you and help carry some of your belongings out."

Together they walked to the parking lot with their hands full of the Beam's belongings, while Debbie and Trevor waited for an orderly to arrive with a wheelchair to wheel the prize patient out the front door.

Troy started the family van and motioned for Paul to jump in the front seat. It was very cold outside, and he wanted the van to heat up completely before Trevor was wheeled outside. The doctor had warned them that Trevor had to be kept extra warm because of his skin graft.

The two men sat in the van and talked as they waited for the temperature to rise in the van. "Troy, I really appreciate the fact that you took time to tell me Trevor's story. I've never heard anything quite like it."

"Well, Paul," Troy said, "as I said to Bill, this has been one blessed experience."

To Troy's surprise, Paul quietly began to weep. With tears in his eyes, he said, "Do you mind if I pray?"

Troy smiled. "Not at all."

The cold winter wind blew snow across the front windshield and ice slowly began to melt off of the windshield wipers that morning as Troy Beam listened to a man talk to God in a way he never had heard before.

"Lord, I've never seen anything like this. I have never seen a man go through what this man and his family have gone through, such a tragedy, and who can then call it 'blessed.' Lord, please give me what he's got."

Troy looked away, toward the driver's side window, and tried to wipe away a sudden stream of tears. It humbled him to listen to that prayer; he felt as if he was listening in to an intensely private conversation between another man and God.

After all, what do I have that is so special, Lord? he prayed silently. *I'm just an ordinary man trying to live my life, raise my children, and be a good husband to my wife. I'm nothing special. The only thing Debbie and I have going for us is our faith in You, Lord Jesus.*

And that was enough. Troy and Debbie had Jesus Christ in their lives; they knew that they could look to Him in times of adversity and even in tragedy as well as in the good times.

When the van had finally reached a comfortable temperature, Troy put it in gear and drove to the front entrance where Debbie and Trevor were waiting, along with a small crowd of nurses and hospital staff.

After Trevor was comfortably settled in the van, Paul turned to Troy with a big smile. He shook his hand and then embraced Troy before he said, "It's been such a pleasure meeting and knowing your family. May God bless you and go with you." With that, the Beams joyfully began their journey home.

It was the first time Trevor had been outside of his hospital room and felt the wind since the Life Lion helicopter landed with his critically injured body just three weeks earlier.

The trip seemed to fly by in a whirlwind of excited conversation, capped by a loud, laughter-laced Beam family reunion when they finally drove up to the family farm.

Later that evening, after they had settled in Trevor and their six other very excited children for the night, Troy and Debbie finally had some private time to pray together.

They knew they had a lot to thank God for. He had literally saved Trevor's life, and then He intervened to supernaturally save his right leg. They rejoiced at what God had done and just marveled at the lives He had touched through their family. Best of all, He had brought their family together again against all odds!

"I know it sounds strange, honey," Troy said, "but this whole experience has been a blessing to me. I feel as though we've been on a three-week missionary trip to the medical center. Every day, God just brought together one thing after another—displays of His healing power; opportunities to bear witness to His grace, love, and mercy; and look at all of the lives that He touched, both inside and outside of the hospital."

Debbie shook her head as she tried to take it all in. "No one but God could have pulled that off. Only the Lord could take such a tragedy and turn it into a triumph."

"Debbie, did you ever feel as if you were watching Scripture being fulfilled before your eyes?" Troy asked. "I keep thinking of that passage in Romans 8:28 that says, *And we know that all things work together for good to them that love God, to them who are the called according to his purpose*."

"Amen," murmured Debbie, half asleep and fully exhausted. Troy smiled tenderly as he gazed at her long brown hair framing her face on the pillow. It had been a long, eventful day following a long month. She had spent so much time and energy keeping home and family going while he spent time at the hospital. Troy leaned down to kiss her, but she was already asleep.

On top of all of that, she is in her second month of pregnancy, Troy thought to himself. *I don't think I could do it...wait a minute—I **know** I couldn't do it!*

He also knew he wasn't quite ready for sleep, even though he also felt totally exhausted.

Trevor's words just kept running through his mind: "You don't know my daddy." Debbie had told him about Trevor's comment to the nurse after she'd told them how the icy conditions from the winter storm was snarling traffic.

As Troy reflected on those words, he was humbled and astounded by the weight and meaning that they carried for Trevor. He always had tried to be the kind of father his children could count on. First of all, that meant to him that he and Debbie always tried to follow through on whatever they said to the children.

"You don't know my daddy."

He was drawn to those words. There was something about them that echoed in his spirit, something that was far larger and greater than himself. *They remind me of my own heavenly Father,* he whispered silently to himself. *That's it—this is about my heavenly Father! I'm learning on a whole new level that I can depend on His Word absolutely, whether it is the written Word that God has given us or the living Word He revealed in His Son, Jesus Christ.*

Troy's thoughts took him to familiar Bible passages he had known and quoted since childhood.

And [Jesus] said, Verily I say unto you, Except ye be converted, and become as little children, ye shall not enter into the kingdom of heaven

—Matthew 18:3

It was enough to make a man rethink his whole life! Troy talked to himself softly, "What would happen if we would just believe the Word of God the way young children implicitly believe what they are told?"

Then it dawned on him. *If we could have the faith in our heavenly Father that Trevor has in his earthly daddy,* Troy reasoned, *wouldn't we all be receiving a lot more blessings in life? Wouldn't we experience joy and peace such as we have never known before? Wouldn't our world be a much better place?*

Troy shook his head and wondered aloud, "If we would simply take God at His word and trust Him, what would happen to our fear and anxiety?"

He was filled with thanksgiving as he considered God's blessings in healing Trevor. Then he prayed, "Father, You know I would have given You the glory whether Trevor had lived or died, but I am so very thankful that Debbie and I did not have to face the loss of a child."

He realized that just as his massaging Trevor's foot made him feel better, so his own Father God's touch on his life was all he needed to feel better. It didn't matter whether he was facing trouble with the business, dealing with the evil that is in the world, or going through the heartache of a son with a tragic injury. No matter what problem he faced, he could go through it knowing that he had a heavenly Father who loved him!

Even after the last 30 days of heartrending trauma that Troy and his wife had endured, he found himself praying softly that night: "In Your hands I have nothing to fear—nothing, Lord. I can look up to You, my heavenly Father, even as my son looks up to me. And just as he knows that I will do all I can to let nothing harm him, I can be confident that You are my heavenly Father and that You will move heaven and earth to take care of me and my loved ones in the same way."

Troy remembered that Jesus posed this question to earthly fathers like himself:

If a son shall ask bread of any of you that is a father, will he give him a stone? or if he ask a fish, will he for a fish give him a serpent?

Or if he shall ask an egg, will he offer him a scorpion?

If ye then, being evil, know how to give good gifts unto your children: how much more shall your heavenly Father give the Holy Spirit to them that ask him?

—Luke 11:11-13

That's the kind of faith Trevor had in his earthly daddy. When the day came for him to leave the hospital, it didn't matter what the nurse or anyone else said based on their knowledge of the circumstances they faced.

Trevor lay back with a contented smile, secure in the knowledge that his father would be there for him. His father had said he would come, so nothing else mattered.

That gave Troy hope, peace, and comfort because he also had a heavenly Father who loved him even more than he loved his son. After all, he served a heavenly Father who gave His Son to die on a cruel cross at Calvary, to be nailed to a cross for him, who exchanged places with him just so that he could be saved.

How much love is that? Troy marveled. *Would I be willing to give up one of my sons even for a friend? Would anyone else give up one of theirs for me?*

Yet, God did. He gave up His Son. He turned His back on Him. On the cross Jesus cried out, *"Eli, Eli, lama sabachthani? that is to say, My God, my God, why hast thou forsaken me?"* (Matthew 27:46).

God had to turn His back on His own Son as Christ bore the sin of the world. He had a plan of salvation for all mankind, and it is there for everyone—for Troy, for Debbie, for each of their children, and for you and your family.

CHAPTER EIGHT

"IT LOOKS LIKE HEAVENLY SKIN TO ME!"

Reality visited the Beam family on Thursday morning, January 31st. The reality of Trevor's being home appeared in virtually every room and routine of the household, and it sent jolts of joy and wonder into every heart in the house.

As usual, Troy was the first to awake that morning—nearly two hours before the sun would finally peek over the eastern horizon. His first order of business was to make his way to the space where he had spent so many heartrending hours of prayer while battling feelings of sadness for nearly three weeks: Trevor's room.

On this unforgettable morning, his father's heart was nearly overwhelmed by gratitude and waves of relief as he gazed at the calm expression of joy on Trevor's face as he slept in his own bed for the first time in 20 long days.

The two oldest boys who rose before sunrise to complete their farm chores normally would have experienced the next encounter with the reality of Trevor's return, but their mother had been waiting for this miracle in her heart and on her knees since the day of the accident.

Unbeknownst to Troy, Debbie had risen almost immediately after him and silently made her way to Trevor's bedside. There she knelt and paused a moment, just listening to the even sounds of Trevor's breathing in a room wonderfully free of the foreign sounds of a hospital. Her own heart seemed to finally step back into its own rhythm after a violent disruption three weeks earlier.

She struggled to hold back the flood of tears that came, then finally gave up. Looking toward the ceiling, she breathed a silent prayer of thanksgiving to the Miracle Worker who saved her son's life and then saved his leg.

"Lord, I don't know what this day or the next may bring, but I know everything is going to work out. Thank You for this morning— for bringing my precious Trevor back home into his own bed in his own room, with his own family. I can never repay You, but I will always thank You."

Debbie had already come and gone by the time T.J. and Trent stood over Trevor's sleeping form, awkwardly wiping away tears and alternately looking at Trevor's face and then into one another's eyes.

Before the accident, they used to wake up Trevor and tell him to hustle so he could join them and do his share of the "man's work" around the farm each morning.

He was the youngest and newest member of the farm team, but he was still an important component of their success. They knew they shouldn't wake him on that first morning, but without exchanging a word in the darkened room, they still shared the same thought: *I can't wait until Trevor joins us again for the morning chores. That is when I'll know that Trevor is really back and healed.*

The boys experienced only a measure of wonder that morning; they were holding the rest in reserve for the morning their personal "normal" finally would fall back into place. It had been during the early morning hours that Trevor's absence became especially painful for them; they ached with hope that he one day would rejoin them for those early morning farm routines that define true "normal" for hundreds of thousands of farming families all across North America and the world.

The Beam boys silently turned around and made their way through the kitchen, put on their coats and work boots, and stepped out of the back door into the deep snow. The animals were hungry and waiting.

The clearest evidence that joy had come to the Beam household was in the change of early morning traffic flow. In the days before the accident, Tiffany and her troop of the three "littlest" Beams usually wandered to the bathroom and then into the kitchen searching for their mother (with Tiffany carrying one-year-old Tiara).

Immediately after the accident, the four-member group had to develop new patterns in a different house since they had spent a good part of the previous 20 days with "Ma and Pa Beam" at their house on the hill. Those were wonderful days with their own special moments, but something always was missing.

On *this* Thursday morning, they had slept in their own beds and rose to all of the familiar sights, sounds, and fragrances that they called home. Plus, there was one *big* difference that morning that made them more excited than any of them could ever remember. Trevor was home.

They were more than ready to welcome Trevor back home all over again on this cold winter morning. Tiffany was the first. She woke up and sat up in her bed almost in the same moment—*Trevor! He's home,* she thought. Somehow the reality of it all seemed even more real this morning than it had last night when she saw Trevor's smiling face in the van after the drive from Hershey.

She skipped the ritual trip to the bathroom to linger outside of Trevor's open door, almost feeling shy about going in to see him. At first she thought he was asleep, but then he popped one eye open and made it obvious to her that he only had been pretending to be asleep!

"I can't believe you did that!" Tiffany said with her hands on her hips in her best imitation of her mother in a "disciplining moment."

"Have you been awake this whole time, Jakey? You just wait— you're gonna get it for that!"

Trevor's face exploded in laughter and his eyes twinkled. He loved to aggravate his sister and best friend! *She makes it s-o-o worth it,* he thought to himself with a smile.

"Tiff, now you k-n-o-o-w I'm not going to change just because of some little accident, don't you?" Trevor said, carefully poking his chest and waving a hand dramatically. "So don't get mad ... hey, where is everybody?" he added, as he craned his neck to see around his sister as she stood just inside the doorway.

Tiffany was trying to think of a smart comeback when her mother showed up carrying chubby-cheeked little Tiara in her arms—with two mischievously shy little faces peeking out from behind her.

"It's about time you got up, Trevor Beam," Debbie said in mock seriousness. "I can't believe that you are gone just three weeks and you come back thinking you can sleep in and be treated like a king or something at home!"

Trevor was wondering if he should feel guilty or not when he noticed her winking at Tiffany. His face lit up with a joyful smile and the whole group of visitors moved closer to his bed.

Debbie had already warned Tiffany and the boys that Trevor would have to stay in bed for awhile until his legs healed, but she still watched Tyler and Travis closely to make sure they didn't jump into Trevor's lap in their excitement.

The tiny details of what followed that morning still stick in Debbie's memories.

She treasured her mental snapshots of the way Tiffany quietly took Trevor's hand in her own and the way the boys just had to touch Trevor's arm. She never would forget the looks of awe and even fear that briefly crossed their faces as they looked at the bandages on his left leg and the exposed raw grafts on his right leg—and how those expressions instantly disappeared in joyful smiles the moment they glanced once more into Trevor's sparkling eyes.

In an oddly detached way, Debbie mentally stepped back from the multiple conversations and delightful sights of the sibling reunion to take in the miraculous nature of what she was seeing.

Only 20 days earlier she had been trying to hurriedly clean up the blood and bloodied scraps of clothing in her kitchen just down the hallway—wondering the whole time if her son would ever return to the house alive, let alone in one piece.

Now here he was, greeting all of them in his own bed with that same smile that had been his trademark almost since his birth! What a miracle!

Tiara brought Debbie "back home" suddenly as she snuggled close to her mommy's neck. As good as it was to see Trevor again, her little girl had her own reality to deal with. She was hungry, and she was already a skilled communicator when it came to the basic needs of life.

Debbie shifted Tiara to her other arm and told Tiffany to stay with Trevor for a few minutes as she steered her little herd toward the kitchen. She knew Trevor would heal much quicker if he could reconnect with Tiffany and reestablish some normalcy in his routine at home.

All that morning as he worked, Troy's mind kept returning to the image burned into his memory of little Trevor sleeping so calmly in his bed. One time he had to stop what he was doing to silently offer a prayer. *Thank You, Lord, for doing what no man could ever do. We'll trust You for what awaits us in the days ahead. Again, thank You.*

Trevor's next appointment with the plastic surgeon who led the Hershey trauma team was scheduled for Friday, February 8th, only eight days away. Several times a day, Debbie and Troy carefully checked Trevor's bandages and changed them when necessary. The skills and procedures they had learned in the hospital seemed to blend seamlessly with the familiar routines of their lives at home.

Due to the extent of Trevor's injuries, the medical team had to take skin from his right leg—the one he had almost lost—to graft onto his left leg, which also had suffered extensive injuries in the accident.

They had warned the parents to be especially vigilant and watch for any sign of infection because the surgeons had decided not to cover Trevor's right leg with bandages. They had to be sure that no more dead or infected skin would have to be removed from the site before they could cover it.

A steady stream of visitors flowed through the Beam house that week as family and friends from several states and churches came to see Trevor. Meanwhile, Troy and Debbie did their best to care for Trevor and reestablish something close to a "normal" life for him. All the while, the upcoming appointment in Hershey was on their minds.

When they took Trevor to see the plastic surgeon at the hospital that Friday, their son's left leg was still raw. They couldn't help but feel anxious as they watched the doctor examine Trevor's leg.

"I'm afraid this skin is not taking," he said, shaking his head. "It will take months for it to heal. The best thing we can do now is do a new skin graft. Once that is done, it should heal in weeks rather than months."

Feeling somewhat discouraged by this setback, Troy said, "Well, you're the expert. If you feel that's what Trevor needs, then let's do it."

The doctor fingered through a worn schedule book to find the note he'd jotted down in his office earlier that morning with a pencil. He put a checkmark in ink beside it before looking up to continue their conversation.

"We'll tentatively schedule the surgery for Tuesday, February 19th; that gives us just over a week to wait to see if anything else happens.

"Tuesday is the day we perform non-emergency procedures. I wanted to get Trevor in earlier, but I'm completely booked next Tuesday. I'll have my nurse call you if there is a cancellation so you can bring in Trevor earlier."

Once again they made the drive home feeling as if something was "hanging" over their heads and delaying the sense of closure they longed for.

A day or two later, while they waited to hear from the doctor if they could move up the surgery, someone from the hospital's financial department called.

"Mr. Beam, our records show that the cost of the skin graft procedure scheduled for your son next week will be approximately $22,000. We simply need to know how you want to pay for that—with cash or a check. It shows here that you have been paying for Trevor's care out of pocket—and that you have no insurance."

"Excuse me, Ma'am. Did you say 'twenty-two *thousand* dollars'?" Troy asked.

"Yes, Mr. Beam, that was $22,000. Would you, er, prefer to wait on the procedure until other financial arrangements can be made?"

"Oh, no. There seems to be no other choice, and the doctor says Trevor needs the procedure. I guess we'll be able to pay for the procedure some way or another. We'll gather the cash for the procedure once we've heard from the doctor on the date he will perform the surgery."

Monday came, but the doctor didn't call—and Troy felt unusually burdened by the situation. *Will Trevor have to wait another week for the surgery? he wondered. Will we all have to dread this thing for another week?*

Finally he brought it to the Lord.

"Lord, there *must* be a reason we have to wait a week and a half instead of just a couple of days for this surgery. I'm trying to accept this, but I just don't understand ... "

And that was when the Lord spoke to Troy's heart with words that transformed his view of the situation and strengthened him with new resolve.

"Son, I am still here. Just ask."

It was late in the day and just about the time when all of the Beam children usually prepared for bed. All of them came into Troy and Debbie's bedroom for Bible reading and prayer, as was their habit. (Trevor was able to move freely around the house in a wheelchair by this time as long as he was careful not to bump the exposed areas on his leg.)

Troy looked at his seven children and said, "God has reminded me that He is still sitting on His throne and that He's still in control. I want us to pray for Trevor's leg and the upcoming skin graft." Then he asked Trevor to lead in prayer.

"Jesus," Trevor prayed, "thank You for saving my life and for healing my leg."

Although he wasn't walking yet, Trevor could move his leg almost normally. He already had told them that he felt that God had already healed him. He took a deep breath and added, "Please, Jesus, heal the skin on my leg, too. Thank You."

The family quickly agreed with Trevor's prayer and sealed it with their own chorus of "amens" and fervent nods before exchanging hugs. Then they went off to bed.

Early the next morning, on Tuesday, February 12th, Debbie and Troy prepared to change Trevor's bandage. They felt especially curious to see how the healing of his leg was progressing after the prayer they had prayed the evening before.

Troy carefully removed the final bandage and then seemed to freeze as he stared at Trevor's leg. Debbie leaned closer and stared down at Trevor's leg in amazement. They looked at one another, then back down again at Trevor's leg.

The whole side of his leg was healed! It had been bloody and oozing the previous Friday, but now it was completely dry. Grafted skin usually has a screen-like appearance because doctors must punch a series of tiny holes in it to help the grafting process.

Trevor's skin was completely smooth.

Troy looked at his wife in disbelief.

"Honey, do you think that's skin?"

"It looks like *heavenly* skin to me!" she answered.

They left Trevor's leg uncovered for an hour just looking at it, comparing it with the skin of his other leg and marveling over what had happened. Finally they decided to wait and re-check the leg in two days, so they re-wrapped the leg and waited.

That Thursday, Trevor's leg still looked as good as it had on Tuesday! Troy looked at Debbie and said, "I think it is time to call the doctor. Why should we spend $22,000 to graft skin onto a perfectly smooth leg?"

It was a morning he would never forget. Once the nurse patched him through to the doctor, Troy described how the entire family had agreed with Trevor's simple prayer on Monday night. Then he explained how they discovered early Tuesday morning that Trevor's leg was completely dry.

"Well, sometimes, Troy, skin grafts can dry up on their own. If it is skin, it is truly a miracle. The only way to know is to carefully examine the skin and check for infection or signs of tissue death. Let's see... Trevor is scheduled for surgery next week if I'm not mistaken..." the doctor said.

"You're the expert," Troy replied, "but I'd like to bring Trevor in and have you take a look at his leg before you actually take him into surgery for the graft next Tuesday."

"All right. I have to say I'm getting used to seeing unusual things happen when your family prays," the doctor said. "I know the costs are mounting up. Come in early and don't go through admitting. That way they won't charge you for the visit."

On Tuesday morning, Troy and Debbie took Trevor to Hershey early for an appointment with his vascular specialist prior to the scheduled skin graft. The nurse explained that if they stayed in the vascular specialist's office after the exam, then the plastic surgeon would come down to meet them there.

When the vascular doctor came in to examine Trevor, he took one look at his young patient and said, "Trevor, you don't even look like the same boy."

One obvious clue might have been the way Trevor was squirming around in his seat. He was as energetic and "fidgety" as any other boy his age who *hadn't* been through what he had experienced.

After that appointment was finished, a plastic surgeon who was in partnership with the surgeon who had led Trevor's trauma team walked into the room. Troy could barely wait while the specialist examined his leg. Finally, Trevor asked, "Is that skin, or what?"

"Yes, that's skin," he replied.

Troy said, "Doctor Boustred talked with me about it last Thursday. He said that a skin graft could dry up like that on its own. He told me, *'If that is skin on there, it is truly a miracle.'"*

Quickly glancing over at Debbie, Troy said, "My wife calls it 'heavenly skin.'"

"Well, it's *definitely* skin," the doctor said, "and *there's no need for Trevor to have a skin graft.*" After he shook their hands and walked out of the office, Troy, Debbie, and Trevor broke out in outright praise and thanks to God. It didn't matter to them whether people in the adjoining rooms heard them or not. *This was another miracle!*

Throughout the whole ordeal with Trevor, every time they had asked God for something—just *asked* Him—He heard and answered their prayers! Every time.

When they tried to explain how they felt to the rest of the family later that night, Troy told them, "We were so excited on the trip home today that we praised and thanked God all the way home! We wanted to thank Him for *everything* He has done, over and over again."

However, everyone in the room was very aware that Trevor was still bound to his wheelchair. Their work of faith wouldn't be done until he was walking.

Later that day Troy told Trevor, "You know, son, God has been so good to you. He has answered every prayer. What would you like to ask Him next?"

Trevor didn't answer immediately. He just sat there with his head down. After a few moments, Trevor looked up and said, "I want to pray that I can walk into my next doctor's appointment."

He was scheduled to go back for an examination of his skin graft on March 7th—only a little more than two weeks away. So his father encouraged him to pray, and Trevor quietly bowed his head.

"Thank You, Jesus, for saving my life and for healing my leg. Now I want to ask You to help me *walk* into my next doctor's appointment with a walker."

As he listened to Trevor pray, Troy was thinking, *No, Trevor, not with a walker; **without it.*** But he didn't say anything because he felt he should respect his son's prayer.

When he talked with Debbie about it later, she felt the same way. If they were going to ask God to heal Trevor so he could walk, why shouldn't they ask Him to heal Trevor all the way so he wouldn't need a walker?

Yet, despite their private misgivings, they felt they should agree with Trevor's prayer and align their prayers with his by faith.

By the week of the appointment, Trevor still wasn't walking and Troy was concerned. "Son, if you're going to walk into the doctor's office on Friday," he said, "then you had better get walking." He even tried to help Trevor stand up and encouraged him to hold onto things and take a few steps, but everything he tried ended in failure. Trevor simply couldn't do it.

Feeling discouraged all over again, Troy turned once again to God in prayer.

"Lord, I guess this is one of those things that is completely in Your hands. Nothing I do is helping Trevor, so I take my hands off and I give him again to You."

After all, he reasoned to himself, *Trevor has made his request. If he is not able to walk on his own into the doctor's office, then it simply means that God had something else planned.*

It was obvious that Troy's attempt to "help" God heal Trevor's leg was useless. He even reconciled himself to the thought that perhaps God didn't want Trevor to walk yet. He sensed this much: He certainly couldn't expect Trevor to wait until the last minute and suddenly walk into the doctor's office on his own.

That Thursday, *the day before the appointment,* Trevor suddenly said, "Dad, would you give me my walker?" And he started walking!

Laughter, loud cheers, broad smiles, and a flood of joyful tears filled the Beam home as Trevor was surrounded by parents and siblings who gathered to watch the miracle unfold.

The next morning, Trevor proudly walked *from the van all the way into the doctor's office with his walker.* It is an understatement to say that he made quite a stir when he entered the plastic surgeon's office. A wide grin lit his face as he greeted the nurse, but she flashed him a smile that easily matched his.

"Trevor, where are your wheels? I can't believe it!"

After giving him a warm hug, she led him *unassisted* into the examining room and went to tell the doctor that Trevor and his parents had arrived for their appointment.

When the doctor came in and saw Trevor standing there with his walker, tears immediately filled his eyes. "Do you mind if I pray?" he asked. Of course the Beams did not mind, and they quickly bowed their heads.

"Dear Great Physician, we know it is totally unnatural for Trevor to be healed so soon and to be walking at all—especially after only two months. We thank You, Lord, for touching his life throughout this difficult situation. Thank You for touching this little boy. It is truly a wonder to see Trevor walking after only two months on a foot that we had no hope of saving—until You intervened."

The doctor shook hands with Trevor, turned to Troy, and said, "Can I give you a big hug?" He then began a clinical examination of Trevor's legs while Troy thought silently to himself:

I didn't think Trevor really would be walking in here today, Lord. I thought You needed my help to get him ready to do this. I guess my faith was just too small. Thank You for causing it to grow, Lord.

CHAPTER NINE

"SOMEONE WORKED ON MY FOOT..."

The doctor told Troy that he wanted to see Trevor again in six weeks' time. When father and son left the exam room, however, there was no one at the reception desk to schedule the appointment.

After waiting for an unusually long time, Troy began to grow impatient. Knowing he didn't owe anything at that point and mindful that Trevor had been standing all that time with his walker, he said, "Come on, Trevor. Let's go home."

While at home, Trevor had improved enough that he could get around on his own fairly well by getting out of the wheelchair and crawling around on the floor. He could pull himself up to the counter and brush his teeth, get a drink, or accomplish other small tasks.

His parents tried to encourage him to do things for himself, even when it was difficult.

"Dad, could you please get me a drink of water?"

"Well, go over and get one. You can pull yourself up."

"But it's so hard, Dad...."

Although sympathetic to his son's plight, Troy knew Trevor needed to help himself so he would not become dependent on others.

"Well, you're just going to have to go do it." And he did it.

When Trevor was still in his wheelchair, before he had begun to walk using his walker, Troy and Debbie had decided to take him to a chiropractor to seek treatment for an ongoing problem with his right foot.

Whenever Trevor moved, his foot dropped down with a small noise. They thought that his foot might be out of joint because whenever he moved it or put weight on the foot, it sounded almost as if the bones were hitting each other.

The only thing they had told the chiropractor was that Trevor had been in an accident. He probably expected the boy to walk in needing to have his back realigned.

"The last thing I expected," he told Troy later, "was to see my new patient in a wheelchair." He examined Trevor's foot and determined that he had a severe sprain. However, due to swelling in Trevor's foot and ankle, he was unable to determine if the foot was out of joint. He asked them to bring Trevor back in a week.

That particular Friday, the day of Trevor's second visit to the chiropractor, was also the day he walked into the hospital on his own in his walker. The hospital and the chiropractor's office were in close proximity, so they had scheduled both appointments for the same day.

So just a week after the chiropractor saw Trevor in his wheelchair, he was surprised to see him walk in on his own two feet in his walker. He expressed amazement at the progress Trevor was making.

At that point Trevor had been complaining for some time of pain in his right foot. Every time he walked on it he felt pain on the bottom of his foot. He never complained of pain anywhere else. It was only when he stood or walked on his right foot that he experienced discomfort.

A friend recommended a massage therapist (the doctor recommended a therapist as well), so Troy and Debbie decided to take Trevor to a therapist about an hour and a half away from home.

On their first visit the therapist placed his hands on Trevor's foot and closed his eyes. He explained that he was trying to feel the tension in Trevor's foot so he could help loosen the muscles.

After his initial examination, the therapist said, "I can't believe this. Despite the tragedy and shock he has been through, he has no aftershock. I would have expected some aftershock, given the trauma and the way in which the foot was injured." Then he added, "I think that within five sessions, one a week, we will see a noticeable difference." And he listed his fee for that first session and for the next five that would follow.

When Tory, Debbie, and Trevor got in the van to go home, Troy looked at Debbie and said, "Honey, not only is God cheaper than that, but He also is a *whole* lot faster!"

He would look into any therapy that would truly help Trevor and consider it well worth it. Nevertheless, the family's budget was also something to think about.

As he continued driving, Troy also continued to think about the massage therapy. The half-hour sessions were very expensive, and on top of that would be the 75-minute drive each week.

Troy considered those factors in comparison with the miraculous healings they had already witnessed and concluded that God could help Trevor the rest of the way, just as He had helped him thus far. Yet, he didn't say anything about his conclusion.

A few moments later on the way home, Trevor looked up at Debbie and said, "Mom, I don't think God wants *man* to heal me. I think *He* wants to heal me."

Debbie smiled. "You know what, Trevor? I think you're right."

Later that evening, as the Beam family got ready for bed, Troy told Trevor, "Son, if you think God wants to heal you, then let's just pray and ask Him to help you walk on your own."

They prayed together and Trevor asked God to take the pain from his foot. Afterward, they went to bed.

Troy was up early the next morning and was downstairs working in his office. Soon Debbie came in with a question. "Did you work on Trevor's foot last night?"

"No, I didn't. Why?"

"Well, I walked in to his room this morning and he asked me if I worked on his foot last night. I told him no and suggested that maybe his daddy did."

But neither of them had massaged or stretched Trevor's foot that night. Debbie went back to his room and asked, "Are you sure somebody worked on your foot last night?"

"I thought so," Trevor replied. "It woke me up. I felt uncomfortable and my leg felt funny. I thought it felt like someone had worked on my foot."

Neither Debbie nor Troy had worked on Trevor's foot that night. But Trevor thought that *someone* had. Had God sent an angel that night?

Although they don't know who may have worked on Trevor's foot that night, the Beams do know one thing: When Trevor got up that morning, he could walk without any pain in his foot. And he has had none since. Trevor walks without any kind of assistance—no walker, no cane—using just the legs and feet God had created and then healed.

God is so good. There are things He does for us that we never know about.

They canceled the next session with the massage therapist. About two weeks later the therapist called Troy on his cell phone. At the time, Troy was perched high in the air putting a roof on a new house.

"Hello, Mr. Beam. I'm calling to ask you how Trevor is doing? The last time I saw him he was still struggling to walk without the walker."

Troy matter-of-factly said, "Thanks for asking. Trevor is doing great."

"Is he walking okay yet?"

"I'd say yes. He's climbing all over this new roof I'm putting on, even as we speak."

At first there was a stunned silence. Then the therapist said, "Excuse me, Mr. Beam. These cell phones just aren't as clear as we'd like them to be. *But did I hear you say 'Trevor is climbing on a roof'?*"

Troy simply said, "Yes."

"Are you sure that it is *Trevor* who is climbing on a roof?"

Troy grinned inside. "Yes. I'm standing here looking at him."

Then the therapist chuckled and said, "I guess, by the sounds of it, that you don't need me."

Troy took that opportunity to tell him about how they had asked God to heal Trevor's foot and help him walk without a walker. When he told the therapist that Trevor believed that someone had worked on his foot that night, Troy could tell by the way the man reacted that he didn't know if he wanted to believe it.

When he described the conversation to Debbie and the family later, he added, "It doesn't really matter to us what anyone else believes or disbelieves. There is one thing certain: We know for a surety that Trevor is running around as if nothing was ever wrong with him! Glory be to God!"

Chapter Ten

"Trevor Defied Every One of Our Expectations"

Several months after Trevor first managed to walk without assistance, the Beams received a phone call from Dr. Boustred at Penn State Hershey Medical Center. He was the plastic surgeon who led the trauma team and who prayed with Troy and Debbie the night of the accident.

After he personally witnessed the miraculous healing of Trevor's leg the first Saturday of his hospital stay, Dr. Boustred began calling the Beams with prayer requests and needs to pass along to "their prayer people." He wanted them to pray because he had seen God working in Trevor's life, and he knew prayers were being answered.

On that particular day, however, the surgeon was calling for a very different reason. He wanted the Beam family to know that he was leaving the central Pennsylvania area to work in a private practice in Colorado.

"Debbie, Doctor Boustred wants to see our family before he leaves," Troy explained while the doctor waited on the other end of the line. "He wants to know if we can come to his office on Friday, June 13th.

That is his last day at the medical center."

After a quick glance at their church calendar, farm calendar, and construction company schedule, they told the doctor they would be there—*all of them.*

On the appointed day, all nine members of the Beam family came through the front entrance of the medical center. Before they knew it, they had drawn a large crowd in the lobby. Staff doctors, nurses, nurses' aides, and support personnel who had trooped through Trevor's room to see "the miracle boy" saw the Beams and couldn't resist getting a personal update on him.

Ironically, very few people actually recognized Trevor because he was walking perfectly well and completely on his own. It seems that the news of their arrival circulated quickly because so many of the doctors and nurses recognized *Troy and Debbie!*

The spontaneous homecoming celebration continued wherever they went in the building. Whether the Beams were walking down a hallway or passing by the cafeteria, someone would walk up to them with an excited grin and extended arms. And most of the time, somebody would have to ask, "Now, which of these boys is Trevor?"

When he grinned at them—and he *liked* doing it—the people all seemed to have the same response: *"It doesn't look like there ever was anything wrong with you!"* Troy and Debbie lost count of how many people they met that day who had worked with Trevor in some way during his three-week stay.

Troy and Debbie were doing their best to herd their family into an elevator when they came face to face with the doctor who headed the Pediatric Intensive Care Unit. He was getting off as the Beam family was filing in, so he reached over to stop the elevator doors and began to talk excitedly.

"I can't even begin to tell you how glad I am that I met you and your lovely family. I think of you and of your son often—especially when we get a difficult case in the PICU."

Then he looked over at Trevor and suddenly realized who it was. A look of marvel and awe seemed to flood across his expression, so the Beams took advantage of the moment to share with him some of the most recent details and miracles that God had done for Trevor and the family.

All of this happened *on the way* to Dr. Boustred's office. When they finally reached it, the receptionist excitedly greeted the Beams and ushered them into the doctor's large office area. Trevor was standing up against the wall when Dr. Boustred walked in, and the doctor immediately recognized him.

"Trevor, walk over here," he said. After Trevor walked over to him, the surgeon said once more, "Now, walk over there, Trevor."

Then he simply shook his head in amazement and said with a broad smile, a shrug of his shoulders, and outstretched hands, "Not even a limp!"

When two other plastic surgeons and a couple of nurses on the hospital staff entered the office, Dr. Boustred motioned toward Troy and said, "Tell them your story." Troy knew he couldn't tell them everything in the short time available to them that day, but he described the first part of Trevor's story.

When Troy reached the point where the trauma team wanted to amputate Trevor's leg, the excitement and anticipation of it all overtook Dr. Boustred and he just had to chime in!

"And that isn't even the half of it. We told Mr. Beam that we really should amputate Trevor's right leg because the leg muscle had been filleted to the bone just as cleanly as someone might fillet a fish!

"We were very reluctant to attempt any reattachment procedures for several reasons—for one, this was a farm accident, and we had no idea just how likely infection might be. But most importantly, as you already know, the long and short fibers of human muscle are intricately interwoven for maximum strength and continuity. However, all of the interwoven texture of the muscle in Trevor's leg had been totally shredded by the violent action of the farm implement he went through.

"Naturally speaking, there was no way this boy's leg muscle should have grown back the way it did. If anything, those muscle fibers would have grown back as scar tissue.

"Even so, he should not have been able to use that leg for at least a year or more. And even then, he shouldn't be able to walk normally because so much of his leg mass *should* be scar tissue rather than muscle."

Dr. Boustred paused for deep breath, smiled, and then looked at the young boy leaning against the wall of the office. *"Trevor defied every one of our expectations.* He defied everything that we predicted."

Before the Beams left his office, the plastic surgeon asked if he could take pictures of Trevor's legs. "I want to be able to show pictures to people when I tell them about Trevor's story—I don't know if they would believe it otherwise!" Dr. Boustred said. "It is amazing, truly amazing!"

So Trevor's story—the story of a Savior who loves us and who still heals and delivers—continues to be shared around the country in doctor's offices, in surgical suites, at nurses' stations, on the Internet, and in countless other ways.

God is good. Trevor and the entire Beam family have moved on, but they have seen God touch many, many lives through Trevor's experience.

Recalling the visit to Dr. Boustred's office that day, Troy said, "I am thankful, too, that we had the doctor we had—a Christian doctor—because that gave us even more peace in Trevor's most urgent hour of need."

Trevor is walking today. In fact, he is running, leaping, and playing as if nothing ever happened to him! What an awesome God!

While Trevor was still in the hospital, his father asked him, "Trevor, do you think you will be able to play football with daddy this summer?"

He shrugged and looked down at his legs as he said, "Dad, I don't know if I will *this* summer, but probably next summer."

Troy happily reports in churches, to strangers, and to news organizations who ask to hear Trevor's story, that Trevor actually played football with his dad even *before* summer arrived! It is at that point that Troy often adds, while doing his best to hold back tears:

"Our son Trevor, whom we feared was dead, is alive and walking today. Not only did God give our son back to us, but He also gave back to us a *complete son,* a son who can walk and who even plays football with me."

One of the most personal blessings Troy describes wherever he goes concerns his relationship with Trevor—a relationship that appeared to have been damaged by the stressful conditions surrounding his birth. In Troy's own words:

"When I told the hospital counselors that the incredible story of Trevor's injury, recovery, and hospital stay was a blessed experience for me, one reason I said it was because of the close bond God created between Trevor and I through it all.

"Before Trevor's accident, I felt at times as if I had no real connection with him. He and his twin, Tiffany, were born at a time when Debbie and I had finally adjusted to parenting a five-year-old and a three-year-old.

"Then Debbie's back 'went out' due to the stress of carrying twins for nine months! I felt badly because she had to endure so much pain, but during that gray period, I was so busy caring for her and the children that I could barely see straight.

"My memory of that time is a blur, punctuated by seemingly endless nights of holding crying babies. As soon as I took one baby to Debbie to nurse, the other would begin to cry. All I wanted was to sleep!

"I just didn't have the same connection with Trevor that I had with my other sons, and I also knew that one-on-one contact and bonding between parent and child is incredibly important to healthy relationships throughout life.

"Ever since Trevor's accident, however, I've enjoyed a deep, two-way connection with my third son. God put us together for three weeks and bonded us together with heavenly cement!

"Sometimes the two of us will be walking in from the barn and Trevor will come up and put his arm around my waist, just bouncing with joy and visibly thankful that God healed him and restored his ability to walk.

"I always will remember the heartache I felt as I watched my little boy for weeks as he sat in a wheelchair and watched the other children play. I knew he was wondering if he ever would be able to join them again.

"Yet even then, Trevor found a way! He is so athletic and so determined that even in the hospital, he actually managed to play tag with other children in his wheelchair! (Remember that at the time, none of us knew whether he would get up and run ever again.)

"God had said He would take care of Trevor, but we didn't know to what degree He would take of care of him or how it all would look in the end. We just asked God to take care of Trevor in His time, in His way, and to His glory.

"Today, Trevor often walks arm in arm with me, secure in the knowledge of his daddy's love and approval. I thank God that we have that kind of blessed relationship now. It is truly a gift from God."

Today, the back of Trevor's right leg looks like muscle with a layer of skin over it. Under normal circumstances, a small layer of fat separates the rugged muscle contours from the surface of the skin and smoothes out the appearance of a person's leg.

Trevor is totally unashamed of his leg. In fact, he calls the appearance of his right leg "God's mark" and considers it to be his public evidence that God healed him supernaturally.

"As for Debbie and I, we look at Trevor and see that his very life serves the Lord's purposes in the same way," Troy explains. "Our son is alive and whole because of God's divine intervention in an impossible situation."

Trevor is whole today, and he is living evidence to any who will listen of what God can do and what He has done for the Beam family.

They publicly praise God for healing Trevor and for giving their family the opportunity to share His love and healing power with people across the United States and around the world through Trevor's song—his astounding testimony of supernatural healing and restoration against all hope.

TREVOR'S SONG

YOU DON'T KNOW MY DAD

My little boy sat there waiting, staring out in the cold.
After three weeks in the hospital they said, "You may go home".
A nurse walked by and told him, "With the roads so bad and all,
Your Daddy may not make it, to take you home after all."

My son, he just stared at her, then he began to smile.
"Daddy said he's coming, and he'll be here in a while.
It might be raining, it might be snowing, and the roads they
   might be bad,
But if you don't think he's coming, then you don't know my Dad."

Chorus

If you don't think He's coming, then you don't know my Dad.
Like my Father up in heaven, the best Friend I ever had.
He sent his Son Jesus, and He'll return again someday,
And if you don't think He's coming, then you don't know my Dad.

This fast world we live in, people seldom stop to pray.
Taking things for granted, only living for today.
God promised all His children, many mansions He has made.
And if you don't think He's coming, then you don't know my Dad.

Written by: **Levi R. Esh**

FINAL WORDS
FROM A MOTHER'S HEART

I often have told my husband that there are two people I *never* would choose to be.

One is a preacher's wife; the other is the wife of the President of the United States. It seems to me that women in both of these positions must deal with enormous pressure to be something or to act as if they are something they really are not—*perfect*.

It doesn't really matter to other people whether or not these women are having a bad day or just "don't feel like being around people" on a certain day. They are expected to perform and pretend as if they are "feeling on top of the world" just the same.

That just wouldn't work for me. Whether other people want to know the truth or not, I do *not* live in a world of perfection and absolute faith. I live in the same world that you do—a world where things can go wrong and where you have some good days and some bad days mixed together.

We often share Trevor's story of God's faithfulness with individuals, churches, and other groups. At times, people will look at us as if we had some kind of super faith or incredible virtue not common among men, but we are just ordinary people who serve an extraordinary God.

The miracle—or actually, the string of miracles—we experienced as God saved our son's life and restored his health did *not* come because we were perfect in our faith or because we had any personal virtue.

We are neither sinless nor special; rather, we are forgiven and loved by a gracious God who openly declares in Romans 2:11, *"For there is no respect of persons with God."*

God loves you just as much as He loves anyone in the Beam family. His Son, Jesus Christ, paid the same price to set *you* free, forgive your sin, heal your body, and bring you hope as He did for *us.*

Trevor walks, runs, and fully enjoys life today because of God's grace, not because my husband or I are such great pillars of faith.

The hard truth is that there were times when our faith ran very low during Trevor's crisis situation. It happened *even* after we had seen some miraculous and inexplicable medical events.

At times, I wrestled with feelings of guilt and condemnation because I questioned whether or not these things were divinely orchestrated. I felt as though I was being a downright sinful skeptic. I thought God must surely be losing patience with me. Yet all I felt coming from Him was kindness, patience and good will. It was almost indescribable. Today, I know I serve a loving God and a Savior who gave His own life to save mine. I think of the great Bible patriarch, Abraham, who is honored for his faith to believe that he would indeed have a child even though he was well beyond child-bearing years. I'm reminded that even that same man who is called "the father of faith" also "sold" his wife to a heathen, idol-worshiping king because he was afraid of him. In other words, he was a painfully human man serving an uncompromisingly supernatural God.

Elijah, the mighty prophet of Israel, called down fire from heaven that was so intensely hot that it even consumed the water that filled the trench encircling the altar.

This same mighty man of faith and power stood his ground alone against 400 pagan priests and publicly proved to the masses that Jehovah was the One True God. Yet, he ran for his life in humiliating fear when Jezebel clenched her tiny, jeweled fists and declared, "I'm going to kill you!"

Why did this powerful prophet fear this little woman? He not only had the Almighty God on his side, but by that time he even had won over the majority of the people as well! Yet, he ran for his life, hid in a cave, and prayed that God would let him die.

In the New Testament, Jesus called John the Baptist the greatest of all the prophets. He was the one who literally saw the Spirit of the Lord descend upon Jesus Christ. Yet, as he lay in Herod's prison awaiting execution, the thing he wanted to know most was something he already had declared to be true to others! He sent his disciples to ask Jesus, "Are you the Christ, the one to come?"

It seems to my husband and I that "ordinary flawed people" are the only kind of people God has to work with. Jesus was the only perfect human He ever had; the rest of us fall short of perfection and will continue to do so until we meet Him face to face.

I remember a conversation I had with one of the hospital counselors during Trevor's stay at Penn State Hershey. I asked him, "What makes you believe there is a God?" At first he gave me the usual answers about his training or studies in God's Word—and all of these are wonderful. But I was probing for something deeper and more personal.

Finally, he said he *really* believed there was a God after he had tried unsuccessfully to *help himself* break an uncontrollable alcohol addiction and the shame it produced. No matter how many times he tried, he failed every time.

Finally, in total desperation, he gave his addiction to Jesus Christ. When he called upon his heavenly Father, then like all good daddies, this man's Father in heaven rescued him.

He said that when he asked Jesus for help, he no longer had to struggle for freedom. His freedom had been purchased 2,000 years earlier by a Jewish carpenter in Israel who loved him.

If you are searching for truth at the foot of a Buddha statue, before a Hindu shrine, or in the house of your ancestors, I want to encourage you to turn your focus upon the Son of God, the One who said, *"I am the way, the truth, and the life; no man can come to the Father except by Me."* [1]

Troy and I had been told while we were growing up that there was a God in heaven who could do miracles and that He loved everyone. We hoped that "everyone" meant us.

When crisis came through our kitchen door, we prayed to that God and had the opportunity to see Him do things for us that is leaving everyone who hears about them in total amazement—including ourselves!

If those miracles Trevor experienced *required perfection* on our part, then we still would be waiting for them. In our dire situation, we came to Him like a child with a broken toy. We simply cried, "Daddy, *help us!*"

The truth is that our backs were against the wall. We had been backed into a corner with nowhere to go but up. And that was where God was. He was just waiting for us to look to Him so He could exert His divine power on our behalf and show us what mercy and grace really mean.

As Troy and I walked together through Trevor's miracle healing journey, God also answered one of our earliest prayers as a married couple—a prayer we prayed right after we had our second child.

Troy specifically asked God for six sons to help him around the farm and with the businesses, and for two daughters. I became pregnant just before Trevor's accident, and at the time we had five sons and two daughters. We didn't know whether the baby I was carrying was a boy or a girl, and we were too pressed during Trevor's ordeal to even think about it or discuss it much. However, we had only one name chosen, a boy's name: Timothy Adam.

To our delight, our *sixth son* was born in September of 2008—fulfilling Troy's prayer in a final and exciting confirmation of God's incredible goodwill toward us!

We are forever grateful to Him for His mercy and grace toward us. The bottom line is that this is not about who we are; it is all about who He is!

Seek God with all of your heart; put your total trust in Him. Take courage and lean on the Lord in every situation. The Bible reminds us, *"For it is God which worketh in you both to will and to do of his good pleasure."* [2]

That means it is God who helps you *want* to do good and who then helps you *do what pleases Him.* That sure explains how He worked in *our* journey of faith.

It seems to me that this takes all of the pressure off of us—and it keeps us from taking credit for what only God can do!

Keep your eyes on Jesus,
Debbie Beam

1. See John 14:6.

2. Philippians 2:13.

With a passion to share God's healing power, His grace and His mercy with the world, the Beam family tells their powerful message of God's love throughout the nation with testimony and music.

Booking Information

The Beam Family may be contacted by writing to:
P.O. Box 104
Newburg, Pennsylvania 17240

or Email them at:
psalm37@innernet.net

Visit us at:
www.thebeamfamily.net
www.trevorssong.com

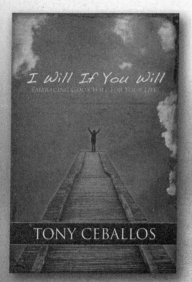

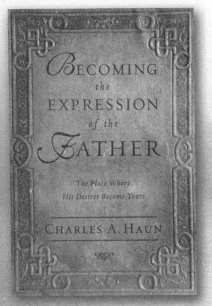

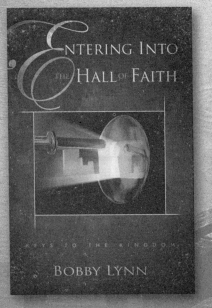
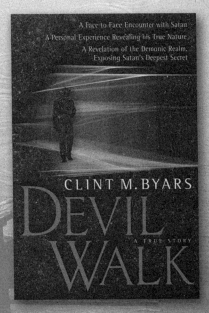

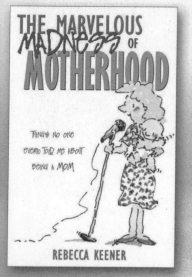

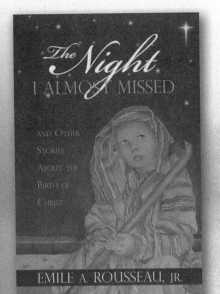
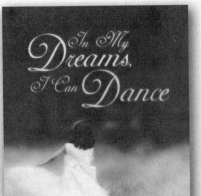
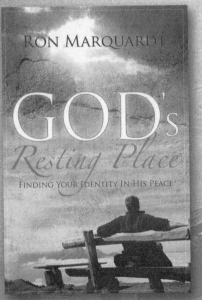